THE CLARENDON BIOGRAPHIES

General Editors: C. L. MOWAT and M. R. PRICE

GLADSTONE

by

E. G. Collieu

OXFORD UNIVERSITY PRESS

1968

Oxford University Press, Ely House, London W. 1

GLASGOW NEW YORK TORONTO MELBOURNE WELLINGTON
CAPE TOWN SALISBURY IBADAN NAIROBI LUSAKA ADDIS ABABA
BOMBAY CALCUTTA MADRAS KARACHI LAHORE DACCA
KUALA LUMPUR HONG KONG TOKYO

*Printed in Great Britain by Richard Clay (The Chaucer Press), Ltd.,
Bungay, Suffolk*

CONTENTS

LIST OF PLATES

1

THE YOUNG CANNINGITE

I

In every generation men of exceptional ability emerge in public life. Once in a century, perhaps, there appears one who transcends all others, dominates his generation, and exerts an influence which long survives him. Such a man was Oliver Cromwell or William Pitt, Earl of Chatham. In the last century, which his life spanned, the greatest parliamentary statesman, and eventual leader of the democracy which he helped to create, was the man who even today is still sometimes referred to, with respect or awe, as Mr. Gladstone. As much a legendary figure as Queen Victoria herself, he embodied a diversity of qualities which rendered him not only unique but also a puzzle to contemporaries, whether they admired or detested him. Today, when the passions which he aroused or shared are largely spent, it is easier than before to appraise this dynamic, controversial figure, and assess his significance.

William Ewart Gladstone was born on 29 December 1809, in Liverpool. Though English by birth and subsequently by education, his ancestry and parentage were wholly Scottish and account for some of his essential characteristics, as well as the northern 'burr' of his speech. His mother was of Highland stock, and from her he may well have inherited the passionate streak in his temperament. His father was a Lowlander who had migrated from the family business of corn-merchant in Scotland to Liverpool, where his energy and enterprise soon established him as a wealthy merchant and leading citizen. He acquired sugar plantations in the West Indies, promoted the election of the liberal Tory George Canning for Liverpool in 1812, and himself became a Canningite M.P. a few years later. From him William acquired a canny business sense, and a lifelong preoccupation with politics.

His career may be said to have started when, at the age of three, he was placed on a chair in Canning's presence, and delivered his first speech, consisting of the words 'Ladies and Gentlemen'.

William was the fourth son in a lively family and passed a happy, uneventful childhood on what was then a rural Merseyside. He was the only one of the children later to achieve distinction, and of this he showed no particular promise in his early years. But his father, now a member of the wealthy and influential mercantile class which could rank itself equal with the older landowning gentry, decided that he should receive the same education as the aristocracy of the day. In 1821 he was sent to Eton, where he spent six happy years, devoted to sport, study, and the making of friends. He found Eton free from snobbery and in later life, when he called it 'the queen of all schools', accorded it a loyal devotion such as he always bestowed upon any place or institution with which he was associated. 'We knew very little, but we knew it accurately' was his verdict on his formal education there. It was, however, at Eton that he was first able to develop two important activities. He became a prominent member of the debating society, and editor of a school magazine. Speechmaking and writing, thus begun, were to remain among his chief occupations for the next seventy years.

He left Eton in 1827, and next year went up to Oxford. His college was Christ Church, closely connected with Eton and the most illustrious in the University. Its members were drawn largely from the aristocracy; it usually supplied one of the University's two M.P.s, and in the course of the nineteenth century it provided nearly half the country's Prime Ministers. Gladstone was to be a good Christ Church man by being both in turn, but to start with showed little likelihood of becoming either. In later life he reproached himself with indolence during his first terms at Oxford. Then his habits changed—for life. Asked in old age to account for his enormous range of knowledge, he answered that he had literally never wasted an idle minute since the age of twenty-one. Now, casting indolence aside, he began to study simultaneously for two final examinations, Classics and Mathematics, and in 1831 he graduated with First Class Honours in both. Thereafter, he ever lived and worked without relaxation under the high pressure of an ambitious examination candidate.

2

The Oxford of Gladstone's day was the unreformed University of an earlier age—socially exclusive, confined to members of the Established Church, whose clergy filled all its offices, politically illiberal in its determination to preserve its privileged position. But it had much to offer to those who were fortunate enough to enter it, and Gladstone enjoyed to the full the many opportunities which lay open to him. As a result, the University not only wrought a change in his working habits but became the greatest formative influence in his life. The brilliantly successful under-graduate who went down from the University in 1831 was a different person from the rather easy-going youth who had entered it three years earlier. He already embodied, in greater or less measure, all the personal qualities and characteristics which marked him for the rest of his life.

His academic success gave evidence of a powerful, disciplined intellect. He possessed an exceptionally vigorous, searching mind and a tenacious memory, which made him a formidable advocate in any issue. He equipped himself to read with equal facility Greek, Latin, French, German, and Italian. His special interests led him to the study of theology as well as the classics, on both of which he wrote and published much; while he always endeavoured to keep abreast of contemporary literature, and enjoyed reviewing new books. Oxford made him an educated man, but he never regarded it as having completed his education. 'I have been a learner all my life,' he said in old age, and he sometimes wondered whether he should not have preferred a life of study to a public career. He regarded Homer, Aristotle, Dante, and the eighteenth-century moralist Bishop Butler as the biggest influences in his life, and he approached nearer to Plato's ideal of the philosopher-king than any other British statesman.

Though he possessed prodigious mental powers, Gladstone was not an intellectual, and was in many respects unsophisticated. The clue to his character, as some observers noted, lay in its simplicity, concealed though this often was by the elaborate and subtle modes of thought and argument which he employed. Like Queen Victoria, he could have defined his whole attitude to life by saying 'I will be good'. This basic simplicity of character served him well and ill. In the course of his career, it was to enable him to make direct, emotional contact with the simple masses of the electorate in a way that no other politician could equal. On the other hand, it often left him at a disadvantage in personal dealings with men of the world and sophisticated poli-ticians at Westminster. Perhaps he never realized, for example, the extent to which his charitable rescue-work among prostitutes could be misinterpreted by the cynical. Gladstone shared the error of many simple men in supposing that what appeared right or good to him must, after explanation, appear equally so to others— the more so, indeed, since his ability to out-talk most men helped him to believe he convinced them. As a result, he was often at a loss to understand why individuals did not respond to him as he expected, or was shocked and indignant at their motives when these differed from his own. At the end of his life he confessed that of all the seventy Cabinet colleagues with whom he had served during half a century, he had understood only one—the conscientious and uncomplicated Lord Aberdeen.

Simple integrity of character and a questing, reflective mind, both reinforced by the influence of clerical Oxford, led Gladstone to embrace religion as the controlling force in his life. The Oxford Movement which, in its efforts to preserve the Church of England, reopened the controversy over the Protestant and Catholic elements in its creed, began after he left the University. But its leaders, Pusey and Newman, were already active figures there, and the issue of Catholic Emancipation, which involved political equality for Roman Catholics, and convulsed politics and public opinion in 1829, had stirred passions in the struggle between the old Tory Anglicans and the new Liberals. This revival of re-ligious enthusiasm seized Gladstone, and the intensity of the con-victions which he formed as an undergraduate became the most powerful driving force in his life. His first inclination, to enter Holy Orders, yielded to his father's advice to think again; and in the end he chose an alternative career in politics. But he brought to this career a compelling sense of vocation which invested his whole life with a unique moral earnestness and elevation, as all contemporaries acknowledged, whether they admired it or thought it hypocrisy. A dedicated Christian, Gladstone sought to conduct his personal and public life according to the precepts of religion, to base his statesmanship upon them, and to see himself as the humble instrument of God's purpose. The first effect of exclusive, Anglican Oxford was to make him a narrow and illiberal churchman; but soon enough his open mind rendered him susceptible to wider and more tolerant influences. He never ceased to be a loyal and devout Anglican—indeed, his sister's acceptance of the Roman Catholic faith caused one of the most painful episodes in his life; but, after his first visit to Rome in 1832, he came increasingly to see England as part of the wider community of historic Christendom, and first its Church, and eventually its people, as members of a common brotherhood.

His formidable combination of qualities would in any case have taken Gladstone far in life, but even so he might have achieved no more than others had not his moral and mental stamina been matched by his physique. When an undergraduate, he could take a twenty-mile walk in his stride, and work twelve hours a day; and only at the very end of his long life did his phenomenal energy and powers of concentration begin to wane. He appeared to be a human power-house, and his commanding figure, crowned by dark hair, white face, and the flashing eyes which uncomfortably reminded many observers of an eagle's, seemed to be engined by an apparently tireless dynamo. When he became a Cabinet Minister in his thirties, a colleague observed that he could accomplish in four hours what would take another man sixteen, and that he also worked for sixteen hours a day. Forty years later, his secretary concluded that his 'horsepower' was at least five times that of any other exceptional man. It was this tremendous reserve of strength, always instantly at his command in thinking, speaking, or writing, which gave Gladstone not the least of his advantages over his colleagues or rivals, and enabled him to pursue a wide range of interests outside politics. It also gave ex-

plosive force on occasion to a naturally impulsive, excitable
nature, of which he was well aware, and which he sought to hold
in check, even if not always successfully. Left fresh by exertions
which would have exhausted or broken others, he found vent for
his overflowing energy in walking, which enabled him to think as
he moved, or in his favourite pastime of tree-felling, which provided the maximum of exercise in the minimum of time. Since he
regarded himself as accountable for his employment of every
minute of every day and lived to attain his eighty-ninth year, his
life was unsurpassed in the range and volume of its achievement.

3

Gladstone's boyhood admiration for Canning inspired him with
an interest in politics which developed spectacularly at Oxford.
He joined the chief debating club, the Union Society, of which he
became President, and soon displayed the oratorical powers which
more than anything else impressed his undergraduate contemporaries. He achieved his greatest success in 1831, when he spoke
in debate against the Reform Bill which the Whig Government
had recently put before Parliament. As a Canningite, he could
appreciate the force of liberal ideas as well as of reactionary Toryism; and since the Reform Bill was designed by the Whigs to
avert revolution rather than to establish democracy, he ingeni-
ously opposed this professedly liberal measure by employing
liberal arguments against it. In later years he was often accused of
sophistry when he resorted to this type of argument; but he made
his debating points triumphantly, and his friends regarded the
speech as an event in their lives. One of them, Lord Lincoln,
recommended him to his father, the Duke of Newcastle, as a
promising young Tory. The Duke had considerable political influence, and the next year agreed to accept Gladstone as his
approved candidate for the 'pocket' borough of Newark where
his influence was usually decisive. By the summer of 1832, the
Whig Government had carried the Reform Bill through Parliament, which was then dissolved; and in September Gladstone
arrived at Newark to start his election canvass. In his addresses to
the electors he demanded the retention of the Established Church

in England and Ireland, and of slavery in the Empire until the slaves had become Christians. At the same time he disturbed the Duke by a reference to the adequate remuneration of labour 'which unhappily among several classes of our fellow-countrymen is not now the case'. He was returned head of the poll in December. The mixture of Toryism, religion, and radicalism in his electoral programme was sufficiently original to suggest an unpredictable political future. In so far as prophecy on this was possible, it had been made already by his Christ Church tutor: 'his conscience is so tender he will never run straight'.

2

THE STERN AND UNBENDING TORY

I

THE House of Commons which Gladstone entered at the beginning of 1833 embodied the results of the Reform Act. This had extended the vote to the propertied middle class, while withholding it from the working class; and it had abolished the most unrepresentative constituencies, whose seats it transferred to a limited number of industrial towns and to the counties. It gave the middle class more influence but no political power; this remained in the hands of the traditional governing class. It was a compromise measure which had averted the threat of revolution, but fell far short of democracy; and it was to remain unaltered for thirty-five years. Although Gladstone was to play a large part in altering it thereafter, he never ceased to admire the system of aristocratic government which the Reform Act preserved, and under which he first rose to political eminence.

The Reform Act had bitterly divided the Whigs and Tories. Though both parties were essentially aristocratic in outlook and composition, they differed in one all-important respect. The Tories were convinced that existing national institutions—Parliament, the Established Church, the Law Courts, the Civil Service appointed by patronage, the magistracy responsible for local government—were fully adequate to provide the country with good government and to carry out all social and economic measures rendered necessary by changing circumstances. They feared that reform of traditional institutions would transfer power from the traditional governing class to the lower classes, whose interests they were otherwise prepared to recognize and provide for. In the previous decade liberal Tories, associated with Canning, had carried out many reforms, relieving Nonconformists and Roman Catholics of their civil disabilities, legalizing Trade Unions, reforming the penal code and the protectionist tariff system. But Toryism remained essentially paternalistic, giving the country partly what it wanted and partly what was considered good for it; and Tories remained opposed to all institutional change which would promote popular self-government.

The Whigs, facing the same problems as had confronted the Tories, were more ready to believe that widespread demand for reforms in a rapidly changing society could best be met by the adaptation of existing institutions or by the creation of new ones. They promoted institutional change to render government more efficient and, to a limited extent, more representative of the new interests which demanded it. Thus, they were willing to concede the liberal principle of popular representation in local government and Parliament, provided it was restricted to property-owners and preserved control at the top in the hands of the governing class. Between 1832 and 1837, they reformed the electoral system of Parliament, and of municipal corporations which they re-modelled; the Poor Law, of which they transferred the local administration from the magistracy to Guardians largely elected by the wealthier ratepayers; and they legalized civil marriage for non-Anglicans. The biggest obstacle which they encountered lay in the reform of the Established Church, and it was on this issue that the Tories, with Gladstone loud in protest, most successfully opposed them.

The General Election of 1832 returned a large majority of Whigs and Radicals which confirmed Lord Grey's Government in power. The Opposition was composed, apart from the small body of Irish nationalists led by Daniel O'Connell, of only some hundred and fifty Tories. These were led by Sir Robert Peel, like Gladstone a Christ Church man with a Double First, and the son of a newly enriched industrialist M.P. He had qualities which led Gladstone first to become his political pupil and finally to revere him as the greatest statesman he had known—immense industry, great parliamentary eloquence, a conscientious determination always to pursue what he regarded as the correct course in politics, regardless of personal consequences. But, deep-sighted rather than imaginative, Peel had nothing in him of Gladstone's impulsive enthusiasm or ardent idealism. Peel's immediate task was to rally his shattered Tory following from defeat and reconstruct the party on a new basis. In less than ten years, it was largely transformed into the new Conservative party which, by adoption of a more accommodating attitude towards public opinion and by exploitation of Whig mistakes, regained the confidence of the country. In the next decade, Disraeli, who then distrusted Peel's leadership, described the new Conservative system as 'Tory men and Whig measures'. The jibe was unfair, but it called attention to the practical element of compromise between reactionary and liberal opinion which Conservatism embodied, and which had to be adopted by most statesmen in the nineteenth century if they seriously hoped to gain or retain power. Gladstone was to discover this hard fact of political life for himself in due course, and often to devote much of his ingenuity and oratory to its justification. For the time being, however, he desired to do little more than oppose the Whigs and all their works, and within six years had earned from the Whig Macaulay the description of 'the rising hope of the stern and unbending Tories'.

2

Early in 1833 Gladstone was elected a member of the Carlton Club, then the unofficial headquarters of the Conservatives. With his impeccable Conservative orthodoxy thus established, he quickly began to make his mark as a promising young member of the Opposition. During the next half dozen years he spoke and voted in opposition to the admission of Nonconformists to the Universities, to the appointment of Nonconformist Chaplains to prisons, to the grant of public money to the Catholic clergy training college at Maynooth in Ireland, to the admission of Jews to Parliament. At the same time he gave his support to the Established Church in Ireland, the retention of Church Rates even when paid by non-Anglicans, the unreformed House of Lords, and the preservation of Negro slavery. He has been criticized so often for his stand on this last issue in particular that it calls for special examination.

The abolition of the Slave Trade in the British Empire in 1807 had been followed by an agitation for the abolition of slavery, which led the Government in 1833 to introduce an Emancipation Bill to free the slaves and compensate their owners. Gladstone's father was an absentee slave-owner in his West Indian plantations, which suffered from a questionable reputation and which he had not allowed his son to visit. When Gladstone opposed the Bill, it was easy to charge him with defending his family's vested interest in slavery. While he rebutted charges of ill-treatment of the Gladstone slaves, his main arguments were on a different plane. He opposed mere emancipation which did nothing to integrate the Negroes into colonial society, and favoured its delay until they had become Christians. Further, since it was notorious that the colonial governments had refused to enact emancipation, he accused the Whigs of interference with colonial rights, in the manner of George III's Ministers who had alienated the American colonies half a century earlier. In thus arguing for colonial constitutional liberty, Gladstone skilfully evaded the issue of personal liberty for the slaves and, by employing a favourite Whig argument against the Whigs, made them appear like the Tories of George III. Gladstone's defence of colonial liberty in this cause may well seem as sophistical as his arguments often did, but it is less easily dismissed as hypocritical. From the beginning to the end of his career, he consistently supported colonial freedom from intervention by the home government. Furthermore, the attitude which he adopted in this case was the same as he took thirty years later, when he supported the Southern Confederacy in the American Civil War against the Federal Government of the North, which he then condemned for wishing forcibly to retain the slave states in the Union against their will. His attitude was again basically the same when, in old age, he supported Irish Home Rule to give Ireland the status of a self-governing colony. In colonial affairs, at least, Gladstone can be seen as a consistent liberal throughout his whole career; but the importance of personal liberty and equality was something he had still to learn.

In 1834, the Government ran into serious difficulty when it attempted to reform the Church in Ireland, and divert some of its superfluous revenues to secular purposes. Two leading Ministers, Stanley (the future Conservative leader Lord Derby) and Graham (later one of Gladstone's closest Conservative colleagues) resigned in protest, and King William IV soon took the opportunity to get rid of the Government. In December, Peel became Prime Minister, at the head of a minority Conservative Government in which Gladstone was given junior office, first at the Treasury and then at the Colonial Office. Aged just twenty-five, he introduced his first parliamentary measure—a Passengers' Bill to improve the conditions on emigrant ships to the colonies. The new Government failed to gain a majority in the existing House of Commons or at the General Election in 1835. It resigned, and was succeeded by Melbourne's Whig Government which lasted for six years. Gladstone retained his seat at Newark and henceforth found himself increasingly busy on Parliamentary Committees dealing with colonial affairs. He was re-elected for Newark in 1837 and in 1841. But by that time he had reached and passed a critical turning point in both his private and public life.

3

When Gladstone came of age and proposed to enter on a political career, his father made him a large annual allowance, and he enjoyed the full independence of a successful young man with a promising future. Before long, however, he found bachelor life unsatisfactorily incomplete, and ardently desired to marry and establish his own family household. Though never a ladies' man in the conventional sense of the term, Gladstone admired beauty and grace in women, and himself had his own masculine share of both these qualities. His high principles and strict sense of propriety, however, at first inhibited him from being a successful suitor, and his rejected proposals of marriage were as dauntingly complex as his more involved political speeches. But in 1838, when on a visit to Rome, he proposed to, and was accepted by, the lovely Catherine Glynne, the daughter of an old Whig family with its country seat at Hawarden in Flintshire. She too had recently been disappointed in love, and protested she had only half a heart to offer him. 'Give it to me and I will make it a whole one,' he replied with desperate brevity. She did, and they were married in 1839 at Hawarden, which thereafter became a home for them and their children until death separated them nearly sixty years later.

Although Gladstone had to labour for years at freeing the Hawarden estate from the debts with which it was encumbered, the marriage was otherwise a cloudlessly happy one. Mrs Gladstone shared and sympathized with all her husband's aspirations, and he reposed complete confidence in her. Where their temperaments differed, she supplied the qualities in which he was deficient. She had a carefree lightness of touch in dealing with people and problems, which enabled him to relax at home and to foster the ordinary human qualities which might otherwise be lost in an austere, dedicated life. Though Gladstone usually had little use for wit, still less for whimsicality, and none for frivolity, his enormous vitality enabled him to enjoy life with zest, and he had a lively sense of innocent fun. His wife and family helped him to release his natural high spirits, and to avoid being solemn as well as serious. Those who knew him only by his public reputation would have been surprised to see him in the nursery, linking arms with Mrs. Gladstone as they uproariously sang about 'a ragamuffin husband and a rantipoling wife' to the children. Hawarden became a haven of peace to which, whether in or out of office, he resorted for as many months as possible in every year, and it was here that he did much of his literary work as well as political business.

It was in 1838, at the time he became engaged, that Gladstone

M.P. for Newark.

M.P. for Oxford University.

OUT OF THE RACE.

GLADSTONE. "PERMIT ME TO EXPLAIN—DEMOCRACY——"
PAM. "OH, BOTHER YOUR EXPLANATIONS! YOU'VE BLOWN YOUR HORSE, AND YOU'RE OUT OF THE RACE."

A BLOCK ON THE LINE.

SUPERINTENDENT BULL. "COME, LOOK ALIVE! I *MUST* HAVE THE RAIL CLEARED. THERE ARE NO END OF TRAINS DUE."

JOHNNY RUSSELL. "IT'S MY JOB, SIR, IF YOU PLEASE."

JOHN BRIGHT. "*HIS* JOB! BEST LEAVE IT TO ME AND MY MATES."

BEN DIZZY. "OUR GANG'LL MANAGE IT, IF YOU'LL LEND A HAND, BILL GLADSTONE."

Competing reformers, 1866–7: Bright, Russell, Gladstone, Disraeli.

A HINT TO THE LOYAL IRISH.

"AH, THIN, MISTHER BULL! GIVE US THE OATH AN' SOME O' THIM STICKS. SURE, THERE'S HUNDHREDS O' THE BOYS AS IS READY TO HELP YE, SOR."

The revival of Irish unrest, 1866–8.

A BAD EXAMPLE.

Dr. Punch. "WHAT'S ALL THIS? YOU, THE TWO HEAD BOYS OF THE SCHOOL, THROWING MUD! *YOU OUGHT TO BE ASHAMED OF YOURSELVES!*"

Gladstone, Disraeli, and the Eastern Question.

published his first book and suffered his first big disappointment. *The Church in its Relations with the State* contained a long and learned statement of his views, which he had often aired at Oxford and in Parliament, on the necessity of preserving the Established Church. Arguing that the State must be Christian and possess a public conscience, he concluded that the British State must maintain the Established Church as the official repository of divine truth in this country against other churches and sects which were in error. The book was warmly greeted by Anglican churchmen, but by few others. Roman Catholics and Nonconformists, as well as Jews and freethinkers, were uninterested in the maintenance of a church to which they did not belong and which enjoyed privileges at their expense; while practically no politician was prepared to flout so large a section of public opinion by supporting such views, even if he privately agreed with them. 'Scarcely had my work issued from the press,' Gladstone recorded later, 'when I became aware that there was no party, no section of a party, no individual person, probably, in the House of Commons who was prepared to act upon it. I found myself the last man on a sinking ship.' He was now compelled to unlearn at least a part of the lesson taught by Oxford clerical Toryism. His sense of the overwhelming importance of religion remained undiminished but, as a responsible statesman, he changed his approach to the problem of preserving it in the national life. If the Established Church was not generally acceptable as the unique agent for maintaining Christianity in the country, then other churches must be enlisted in the task, and their convictions recognized. This must inevitably lead to religious freedom and equality—both of them liberal policies previously anathema to most Tories.

Great though Gladstone's disappointment was at the collapse of the policy which he had cherished for ten years, the failure was nothing but salutary. It helped him to escape from the most rigid and intolerant article of the old Tory creed, which had hitherto arrested his political development, and to make broader contact with the new liberal forces which were influencing public opinion and a growing section of the Conservative party. Within a few years he was to distress his father by voting for the admission of Jews to Parliament. The change of attitude towards religious toleration, which the rebuff of 1838 started in him, soon coincided with a new turn in his career that was to carry him yet farther towards liberalism.

4

In 1841 Melbourne's Whig Government finally collapsed, and at the General Election the Conservatives were returned with a majority. Peel became Prime Minister and appointed Gladstone Vice-President of the Board of Trade. This was a wise choice, but at first Gladstone was indignant and mortified. He had hoped for the Irish Secretaryship which would enable him to administer the most troubled part of the United Kingdom according to his idealistic principles of religion and political philosophy. 'The science of politics,' he complained, 'deals with the government of men, and I am set to govern packages.' It was the sincere objection of an idealist who always felt that 'politics are too much immersed in matter' to be entirely congenial. But Peel, who recognized Gladstone's great potential ability and thought he needed to be brought down to earth, was firm. Protesting that he was 'totally ignorant of political economy and of the commerce of the country', Gladstone now set about mastering both with conscientious thoroughness at the Board of Trade.

He could hardly have been appointed to a more important office than this at the time. If Ireland appeared to be on the verge of revolution as O'Connell led his national agitation for the repeal of the Union, England also seethed with discontent and violent unrest. This was the period of the 'hungry forties', when the whole political and social system of the country was under fire from the under-privileged classes. The working class, denied the vote by the Reform Act, suffered from widespread unemployment, low wages, intolerable conditions of work in mine and factory, a harshly inadequate system of poor relief, and a large measure of neglect in housing and education. These evils gave rise to the Chartist Movement which, in the People's Charter repeatedly presented to Parliament, demanded the creation of a political democracy such as exists today. The middle class, though represented in Parliament, was excluded from political power by the dominant aristocracy, whose monopoly of all important offices in Church and State it resented. Mainly engaged in commerce and industry, it increasingly attributed the economic depression to the protective tariffs which comprised the country's fiscal system, and especially to the Corn Laws. These imposed an import duty on corn which, it was alleged, artificially raised the cost of bread at the expense of the people, for the advantage of the landowning aristocracy and gentry whose farm-rents alone benefited from it; while it impeded the purchase of corn from foreign countries which otherwise would be able to buy British exports in exchange. A great national organization, the Anti-Corn Law League, was formed to secure the promotion of free trade in foodstuffs and other articles. The agitation was led by two Radical M.P.s, Richard Cobden and John Bright, and soon appeared as dangerous to the Government as the Chartists.

Gladstone, disapproving like most Conservatives of both movements as unconstitutional in their attempts to put pressure on Parliament, set about mastering the facts of the issue beween Free Trade and Protection. Within a few months he had done so and become a convinced Free Trader. He assisted the conversion of Peel who, in 1842, reintroduced the Income Tax and, thus provided with a revenue from direct taxation, began the progressive reduction or abolition of many import duties on raw materials, manufactured goods, and foodstuffs. The assistance which Gladstone gave him was so valuable that in 1843 Peel made him President of the Board of Trade and a member of the Cabinet. It was in this capacity that, in 1844, Gladstone secured the enactment of his first great measure, the Railway Act, which imposed a code of regulations upon the new railways spreading over the country, and provided for their possible nationalization at a later date. It is characteristic of his open-mindedness in policy that while he worked for the reduction of state intervention in trade he could envisage its extension in transport.

The next year, 1845, was one of crisis for Gladstone and the whole Conservative party. The Government, which had quelled

O'Connell's nationalist agitation, sought to conciliate Irish opinion by increasing its annual grant to the Catholic training college at Maynooth. This meant that, while it maintained the established Protestant Church of Ireland, it undertook an extended 'concurrent endowment' of the unofficial Catholic Church. As the latter ministered to the great majority of the Irish, the policy was one of justice as well as appeasement. By now Gladstone personally agreed with this policy, but six years earlier he had publicly committed himself to the opposite view that the State should support only the State church. He felt obliged in honour to resign from the Government, lest he should appear as a time-serving office-holder who compromised with his convictions in order to assist his career. His conscience was, indeed, so tender that when he explained his reasons for resignation in the Commons his speech was not understood by anyone.

As a disinterested private M.P. again, Gladstone voted for the Maynooth Bill, but many Conservatives voted against it. Opposed to Irish nationalism and Roman Catholicism, and distrusting the Government's increasingly liberal economic policy, they were beginning, with Benjamin Disraeli as their spokesman, to revolt against Peel's leadership and his departure from much of the old Tory creed. The final crisis came at the end of 1845. By then it was clear that the Irish potato crop, upon which the majority of Irish depended for subsistence, had been destroyed by disease, and that Ireland faced famine. Peel, who had hitherto avoided committing himself to the abolition of the Corn Laws, for fear of splitting his party which largely represented the landed interest, now decided to make the Irish famine an excuse for securing the free importation of corn. Though this would not help the Irish peasants, who were too poor to buy corn, it would put an end to English discontent embodied in the Anti-Corn Law League. The Whig leader, Lord John Russell, declared in favour of Free Trade, and Peel, anxious to preserve his party's unity and his own reputation as its leader, resigned. When, however, Russell failed to form an alternative Government, Peel returned to office with a new Cabinet committed to Free Trade in corn.

Lord Stanley (later Lord Derby) refused to enter the Government, and thereafter led the majority of the party in opposition to Peel. But Gladstone readily joined it, and was appointed Secretary of State for War and Colonies. Under a law which existed till the present century, Ministers on appointment had to seek re-election to the Commons. The Duke of Newcastle was a firm Protectionist and would not put Newark at the disposal of a Free Trade Conservative. Gladstone, therefore, could not secure re-election and, though he retained his office, was out of Parliament for the next year and a half. By June 1846 the Bill abolishing the Corn Laws was carried through Parliament, the Opposition voting for the Government, and most of the Conservatives voting against it. Then the Whigs joined with some Protectionist Conservatives in united opposition to Peel and forced his resignation. Russell formed a Whig Government, which proved to be the last such in English history and which, with the support of the Peelite Conservatives, lasted for six years. Nearly thirty years were to pass before there was again a Conservative party majority in the Commons.

3

LIBERAL CONSERVATIVE OR
CONSERVATIVE LIBERAL

I

GLADSTONE's short tenure of the War and Colonial Office, without a seat in Parliament, did not enable him to achieve much, and he welcomed its end. Though often regarded as ambitious for office, probably no other statesman so often declined it, or resigned, or threatened to resign, from it. 'And now,' he joyfully wrote in the summer of 1846, 'goodbye Council, goodbye representative institutions, goodbye all Emigration and Immigration except the emigration of out-of-office Parliament men from town in this dying season and their immigration into the country.' Except for a short period, he was to be out of office for the next dozen years; and meanwhile his political re-education continued. He now belonged to the Peelite group of liberal Conservatives, and had progressively to redefine his apparently self-contradictory position.

He re-entered Parliament at the General Election of 1847 as M.P. for Oxford University. This constituency, which consisted of the University's graduates, was in many ways attractive. He felt a loyal and sentimental attachment to Oxford, and found its preoccupation with ecclesiastical and educational affairs very congenial. But his political connexion with it was a mixed blessing. The University, with its privileged and restricted membership, was not yet a genuinely national institution, and provided in some ways even less of a popular constituency than the Duke of Newcastle's Newark. It offered few opportunities to any politician who might hope to become a national leader.

There was in Oxford, however, a growing body of liberals who sought to reform the University, and increasingly looked to the Government to assist them. When, in 1850, Russell appointed two Commissions to investigate the ancient Universities, Gladstone opposed this intervention by the State in what was regarded as the preserve of the Anglican Church. But within three years he had been won over by the liberals, and not only accepted the major recommendations of the Oxford Commission, but did much to implement them. These not only changed the constitution of the University and rendered it more efficient as an educational institution, but also made possible the admission of non-Anglicans —though these could not acquire higher degrees or University offices until Gladstone's first Government relieved them of this final disability nearly twenty years later.

In 1846, Gladstone had been well placed at the Colonial office. As Free Trade destroyed the old colonial system of protection which gave low tariff preference to colonial exports to Britain, the colonies desired a greater measure of freedom to control their fiscal policies for themselves. During the Parliament of 1847–52, he generally supported the Whig Government's measures for the extension of colonial self-government, notably in Australia and New Zealand, for which new constitutions were enacted. In this way, the liberal principles of Lord Durham's famous Report, issued after the Canadian rebellions of 1837, were implemented and extended. Gladstone was always fearful lest restrictive government by the mother-country should provoke the colonies to rebel and leave the Empire, as the United States had done. He emphasized his conviction that, while the mother-country must protect the young colonies until they could protect themselves, nothing should be done to impede their development towards individual nationhood, or even independence if they should desire it. This later gained him the reputation of being an unpatriotic 'little-Englander', which he was not. Rather, he hoped that every colony would voluntarily become a 'new England'. He envisaged the transformation of the Empire into a Commonwealth, such as was created in the present century, in which colonies would remain freely attached to the mother-country by ties of sentiment, culture, interest, and the possession of the same religious and political institutions. 'We cannot,' he said, 'stamp the image of England on the Colonies like a coat of arms upon wax. For all true, genuine, wholesome and permanent resemblance, we must depend upon a law written not upon stone but on the fleshy tablets of the heart. It must be wrought wholly through the free will and the affection of the colonial community.'

The colonies which roused Gladstone's concern were primarily the great 'colonies of settlement', in Canada, Australasia, and South Africa, created by settlers and emigrants mostly of British stock. For the rest of the Empire—the 'colonies of exploitation' which were territories often acquired or retained for profit or prestige, and unsuitable for white settlement—he felt far less concern. Here he was an anti-imperialist. Opposed to the extension of the British Empire by conquest, or its maintenance by oppression, he came to dislike or distrust all empires which resorted to such means, and opposed the wars to which they gave rise. Thus, his interest in imperial policy fostered a growing interest in foreign affairs, and quickened his religious concern with the morality of war as an instrument of policy.

2

Except for the years 1834–5 and 1841–6, when Conservative Governments were in office, Lord Palmerston was the Whig Foreign Secretary from 1830 to 1851. A former Canningite, Palmerston was successful and popular in the country as a vigorous champion of British interests abroad. His practical interpretation of these led him frequently to encourage liberal or nationalist movements in Europe, especially within the Austrian Empire, and to rely upon 'gun-boat diplomacy' in enforcing British demands upon weaker states elsewhere. His methods did not go uncriticized, especially by Queen Victoria who finally secured his dismissal in 1851. By that time, Gladstone had come to consider him, as did the Queen and Prince Albert, a bully who damaged Britain's reputation with foreign governments. He clashed notably with Palmerston in 1850; then the Government was attacked in Parliament for sending a naval squadron against Greece, because the Greek Government would not pay exorbitant damages claimed, after a riot in Athens, by a resident named Don Pacifico, who was technically a British subject. Unjustifiable though the action was, Gladstone's indignant and sarcastic eloquence could not prevent the popular Palmerston from gaining a vote of confidence.

In another sphere, however, Gladstone was to find an unexpected ally in Palmerston. The year 1848 was one of violent political unrest or revolution in Europe. At home, there was an abortive rising in Ireland, and a monster demonstration by the Chartists in London, where Gladstone enrolled as a special constable. Most European capitals were swept by revolutions which were suppressed with difficulty. One of the States most severely affected was the Austrian Empire which, for a year, lost control to liberal or nationalist governments in Hungary, the German Confederation, and the Italian peninsula where, since 1815, its influence had been supreme. In 1850, when the old order had been ruthlessly restored, Gladstone paid one of his many visits to Italy and investigated the conditions of political prisoners in Naples. He was horrified by his discoveries. On his return to England in 1851, he wrote to Aberdeen, whom he regarded as Conservative

leader since Peel's death in 1850, denouncing what he called 'the
negation of God erected into a system of government', and urging
Conservatives to remove a cause for reproach which must otherwise stain their reputation. Much embarrassed by this outburst on
behalf of liberal revolutionaries, Aberdeen could take no effective
action. Losing all patience, Gladstone further embarrassed his
Conservative friends by publishing his letters to Aberdeen. These
created a sensation, and Palmerston had copies distributed to
every Court in Europe as an expression of British opinion on the
Italian question. Thus, Gladstone found himself regarded as a
liberal in foreign policy, and three years later he was finally converted to the cause of Italian nationalism, in the struggle to expel
Austrian rule and unify Italy.

Liberal since 1833 in colonial policy, since 1842 in fiscal policy,
and now increasingly sympathetic towards liberal principles in
religious and foreign policy, Gladstone had moved in twenty
years from the right to the centre in politics. Though still a Conservative, he had established too many points of contact with the
Whigs and the liberal movement in the country to permit his
easily rejoining the main Conservative party under Derby. In
February 1852, when defeat drove Russell to resignation, Derby
became Prime Minister and formed a Conservative Government
which he invited Gladstone to join. The party was in a minority
in the Commons, and Gladstone declined to join what looked like
being a weak, Protectionist Government. Instead, Disraeli became
Chancellor of the Exchequer and its leader in the House of
Commons, and thus began the political rivalry between the two
men which lasted thirty years. In December, Disraeli produced
his Budget, which was condemned by Gladstone, for its disregard
of Peel's principles, in a speech so devastating that the Government was defeated and at once resigned.

As no political group or party—Whigs, Conservatives, Peelites,
or Radicals—possessed a majority since 1846, only a coalition
could provide a stable Government. The Queen appointed Aberdeen Prime Minister with a Cabinet composed of Whigs, Peelites,
and one Radical. On her advice, Gladstone was appointed Chancellor of the Exchequer. In this coalition was laid the foundation

of the later mid-Victorian Liberal party, and of Gladstone's reputation as a finance minister. His first Budget, introduced in 1853 in a House of Commons which listened enthralled by his five-hour speech, was one of the great events of Victorian politics.

3

Gladstone was the greatest Chancellor of the Exchequer in the century, not only because he acquired an unequalled grasp of public finance, but also because he employed it as an instrument which influenced government in all branches of policy and administration, as well as the nation's economy and social development. By his work at the Treasury he gradually made the office second in importance only to the Premiership, and he attained exceptional influence when he occupied it. Though he called some of the work 'dry and repulsive', he mastered it all, from first principles to the smallest details, with single-minded enthusiasm, and expounded his Budgets in speeches in which, wrote a contemporary journalist, 'he talked shop like a tenth Muse'. His own recipe for a financial speech was deceptively simple: 'Get up your figures thoroughly and exhaustively, so as to have them absolutely at your fingers' ends, and then give them out as if the *whole* WORLD was interested in them.' He now gained the attention of the whole country, and for the first time tasted the delights of almost universal popularity.

The Budget of 1853 opened Gladstone's long campaign for fiscal, financial, and economical reform, and embodied many of his working principles, partly inherited from Peel and partly his own. These were few but effective. First, Free Trade was to be expanded by reductions in the tariff upon imported industrial goods and materials, in order to cheapen costs of production and so stimulate the expansion of industry, and upon articles of common consumption, especially foodstuffs, in order to lower the cost of living. Second, all small taxes which cost more to collect than they produced in revenue must be abolished. Third, taxation should be spread as equitably as possible, to relieve the poorer classes least able to pay them. Fourth, government expenditure should be reduced as much as possible, to permit a reduction in taxes which would leave more money at the taxpayer's disposal for investment as well as expenditure. Fifth, government services should be rendered as economical and efficient as possible, to give the taxpayer best value for his money. To begin with, in 1853, Gladstone removed 123 articles from the tariff, and lowered the duty on 133 others. To make good the consequent loss of revenue, he secured the passage of a Succession Duties Act which taxed inheritance of property, and the temporary renewal of the Income Tax, with a view to its abolition in 1860. But at this point, his financial programme was abruptly disorganized by external events.

The greatest single part of the Empire was India, the routes to which, before the opening of the Suez Canal in 1869, passed through the Turkish Empire. It was a prime object of British policy to preserve Turkey from aggression by Russia, which was regarded as a danger to British interests in Asia. In 1852 France, now ruled by the autocratic Napoleon III, made claims on behalf of Roman Catholics in the Turkish Empire which were opposed by Russia. Turkey failed to satisfy the counter-claims made on behalf of the Orthodox Church by Czar Nicholas I, who occupied the Turkish border provinces with troops as a 'material guarantee' of Turkish good behaviour towards Russia. Much of 1853 was spent by the British Government in anxious consultation with all the powers concerned. A diplomatic solution of the problem was peacefully reached, but Turkey finally refused to accept it. A Russo-Turkish war then broke out, and went so badly for Turkey that Britain and France entered it as her ally in 1854. A large Anglo-French army invaded the Crimea in order to capture the Russian fortress-port of Sebastopol on the Black Sea.

Gladstone believed the war to be just because necessary to compel Russia to observe the rules of international law, though he may not have been convinced that Russia was the only aggressor. His attitude was reflected in his Budget speech of 1854 when, raising the Income Tax from 7*d*. to 1*s*. 2*d*. in the £, he said, 'The expenses of war are a moral check, which it has pleased the Almighty to impose upon the ambition and lust of conquest that are inherent in so many nations.' In the same mood, he later increased other taxes, rather than rely on the easier but more expensive method of borrowing money to finance the war. By the beginning of 1855, the British Army had failed to capture Sebastopol, and had been nearly destroyed by the Crimean winter for which it was not prepared. Public indignation at mismanagement of the war was so great that, when a Parliamentary Committee of Enquiry into it was proposed, the Government resigned. Eventually Palmerston was able to form a new Government which Gladstone reluctantly joined, only to resign a fortnight later. He would not accept the Enquiry, and he could not approve of the war which Palmerston seemed anxious to carry on until Russian power was broken. He was opposed to an imperialist war, as he considered it to have become, and in later life said that the greatest mistake in his career was to have helped make possible a Palmerston Government in 1855.

Gladstone now became as unpopular as he had recently been popular, and soon appeared as an isolated figure, equally out of touch with all parties and with the electorate which backed Palmerston. He was, said a contemporary observer, the most powerful speaker and the weakest man in the House of Commons. He passed the next four years in the political wilderness, where he often appeared to be in opposition to everyone and everything. He criticized every Budget; he courageously denounced armed intervention in China; he strenuously opposed the Act establishing a general Divorce Law in 1857, when he exploited parliamentary debating procedures, of which he was a master, to obstruct what he considered an irreligious and ill-founded measure. He found more satisfaction in personal activities outside Parliament. Throughout these years he gave public lectures on the colonies and on foreign missions, and published articles on a variety of topics. In 1858 he published his second big book, *Studies in Homer and the Homeric Age*. This labour of love failed to gain much acceptance by professional scholars, and perhaps shed as much light upon Gladstone as upon Homer.

Just before the book appeared, Palmerston's Government, which had triumphantly won the General Election of 1857, was unexpectedly defeated in the Commons, and resigned. Derby again became Prime Minister and again invited Gladstone to join his Conservative Ministry. Again he declined. His dislike of Disraeli as an unscrupulous destroyer of Peel has usually been regarded as the obstacle to his acceptance, though Disraeli had offered to resign the Conservative leadership in the Commons in his favour, and Gladstone gave as his own reason the general distrust or dislike of the Conservative rank and file for himself. Later in the year, Derby was able to relieve him of his embarrassing position by appointing him temporarily High Commissioner in the Ionian Islands, a British possession which now wished to join Greece.

Gladstone returned to London in 1859, and resumed his ambiguous political position—but not for long. At this point, the small Italian state of Piedmont went to war with Austria and, aided by a large French army, started to drive the Austrians out of north Italy. The Conservative Government, still in a minority, was hostile to the popular Italian movement, and was soon obliged to resign. Gladstone voted for it in a last, unsuccessful effort to save it from defeat, and then accepted an invitation from Palmerston to become Chancellor of the Exchequer in a new Liberal Government. Thus incongruously did he enter the Liberal party which he was increasingly to dominate for the next thirty-five years.

4

Palmerston's Cabinet was composed of Whigs, Peelites, and one Radical. The Foreign Secretary was Russell. He and Palmerston were called 'the old Italian Masters', and active sympathy with Italian nationalism was almost the only political interest which Gladstone had in common with them. The Government's benevolent attitude helped Piedmont to liberate and unite the greater part of Italy in a new state within a year; but serious divisions arose within the Cabinet even before this common factor had ceased to operate. Napoleon III, who had led his army against Austria on Piedmont's behalf, obtained the province of Savoy as his reward, and quickly revived British fears of French aggrandisement. Gladstone believed these fears to be unfounded, and when Palmerston proposed a large programme of rearmament, he sought to limit this by reductions in its cost.

The Budget of 1860, therefore, resembled that of 1853 and not that of 1854, and Gladstone regarded it as his greatest. He retained the Income Tax, which he had once planned to abolish in this year, but only to enable him to cut down the remaining protectionist tariff. He reduced the duties on imports from 419 to forty-eight, of which only fifteen produced a large revenue. At the same time, he encouraged Cobden, whom he no longer regarded as an unconstitutional agitator, to go to Paris and negotiate a trade treaty with France, in the hope of relaxing international tension. In the end, there was no war with France, though Palmerston was able to carry out a modified rearmament programme. Gladstone contested this at every stage in the Cabinet, often alone in his opposition to it, before he secured a compromise. 'Gladstone doesn't convince you that he's right, but he does convince you that you're wrong,' complained one Minister. He threatened resignation, but this could not be accepted, since the rapidly increasing prosperity of the country, which his Budgets stimulated, made him popular among all classes. The Budget was brought below £70,000,000 a year and, while the levels of Government expenditure and of taxation fell, trade figures soared. His object was not only to lower taxation and the cost of living, but also to expand production and particularly employment. As he achieved these ends he came to earn the good opinion of the Radicals and working-class leaders, to whom he increasingly looked for support against his colleagues. He gained popular approval when he secured the abolition of the duty on paper in 1861, against the wishes of the House of Lords, and in 1863 when he established Post Office Savings Banks to assist the thrifty small investor. In 1861 he established the Public Accounts Committee in the Commons as a check upon wasteful public expenditure, and in 1866 secured the creation of the office of Comptroller and Auditor-General to promote economy and efficiency in government spending.

While prosperity and social peace took deeper roots at home, wars raged in most of the world outside. In Europe, the German nationalist movement was as active as the Italian. In 1863-4, Austria and Prussia fought Denmark, to liberate two Danish provinces which contained German-speaking inhabitants. Palmerston and Russell favoured intervention to preserve Denmark, in the British interest, but Gladstone was not convinced and joined the non-interventionist group in the Cabinet. This finally prevailed, partly as a result of Queen Victoria's determination to assist the German nationalist movement, and Gladstone gratefully acknowledged the value of her intervention to keep the country out of the war. Though the defeat of Denmark was prelude to the Austro-Prussian war of 1866 and the achievement of German unification under Prussia in 1870, the Government meanwhile had a more serious preoccupation across the Atlantic, where Canada required the British army to protect it against possible attack. In 1861 began the American Civil War, which nearly involved Britain. Popular opinion in England supported the Federal Government of President Lincoln as democratic and opposed to slavery; but Gladstone, like the majority of aristocratic Society, favoured the cause of the Southern states which he thought should be allowed freely to secede from the Union. The Southern Confederacy purchased armaments in Britain, notably the armed privateer *Alabama* which destroyed so much Federal shipping that Anglo-American relations were severely strained for years to come. In 1862, Gladstone greatly embarrassed the Government by publicly praising the Southern Confederates—an act of 'incredible grossness', as he later confessed. After the war, he came to respect and admire the reunited U.S.A.; and it was Gladstone whom the future President Wilson later took as his model statesman.

One result of the war was the loss to British industry of imports of raw cotton from the Southern states. Unemployment and distress were widespread, especially in Lancashire where Gladstone supplied relief by a government loan. In 1862 and 1863 he visited the North Country to see conditions for himself, and was deeply impressed by working-class morale in adversity. Instead of the old revolutionary spirit of Chartism, he found orderly Trade Unions, thriving Cooperative Societies, and an eager interest in political issues which concerned himself. Equally important, he discovered that on the public platform he was an outstandingly successful speaker to whom the large popular audiences enthusiastically responded. Much impressed by what he called their 'little tutored yet reflective minds', he began to sympathize with working-class political aspirations, and drew closer to the popular Radical leader Bright, who distrusted Palmerston even more than he did. In 1864, Gladstone stated in the Commons his new-found belief that 'every man who is not presumably incapacitated by some consideration of personal fitness or of political danger is morally entitled to come within the pale of the constitution'. This unheralded admission of his latest political conversion reopened the issue of parliamentary reform.

Palmerston, who had occasion to regard Gladstone as disloyal to him, was embarrassed by this statement which, without previous warning or discussion, appeared to commit the Government to the principle of democracy. Now aged eighty, he desired only to let sleeping dogs lie and, in collusion with Derby, to maintain the old aristocratic system unaltered. Apart from Gladstone's financial measures, the Government had no achievements to its credit, and hardly desired any. The popularity of Palmerston and Gladstone with different sections of the small electorate enabled the Government to win the General Election of 1865, but this was the last success of the old order. Gladstone, now unquestionably a Liberal and in apparent alliance with popular Radicalism, was no longer able or willing to remain M.P. for Oxford University. 'He is a dangerous man,' Palmerston had said. 'Keep him in Oxford, and he is partially muzzled; but send him elsewhere, and he will run wild.' Defeated at Oxford, he secured election for South Lancashire, to whose electors he announced, 'I am come among you unmuzzled.' Three months later Palmerston, and with him the early Victorian era, died. Russell was appointed Prime Minister, and Gladstone became the Government's Leader of the House of Commons. Fortunately for himself, Palmerston was spared seeing the speedy realization of his prophecy that 'Gladstone will soon have it all his own way; and whenever he gets my place, we shall have strange doings'.

Top: Tree-felling at Hawarden.   *Above:* Gladstone, Hartington, and Chamberlain.

"THE START".

(GREAT RACE BETWEEN THE G.O.M. AND "THE MARKISS".)

THE "OLD UMBRELLA"!!

The last public appearance, 1896.

Top: The Cult of the Grand Old Man.
Above: At work in retirement, 1896.

4

THE PEOPLE'S WILLIAM

I

RUSSELL, one of the architects of the first Reform Act, was anxious to achieve a further measure of parliamentary reform before his career ended. In 1866, the Government introduced a Bill which lowered the property qualification for the vote, and at once encountered serious difficulties. A party elected to support Palmerston was a poor instrument for reform, and the efforts of Gladstone, as leader in the Commons, to secure its unity on the issue proved inadequate. A group of dissidents, led by Robert Lowe, joined the Conservatives in defeating the Bill, and the Government resigned. Derby now formed his third Government, with Disraeli leading it in the Commons; and while they laid their plans for the next session, Gladstone, mortified by his recent failure, went off to Italy.

Though the Conservatives were in a minority, Disraeli was determined to succeed where Gladstone had failed, and did so—at a price. When, in 1867, the Conservatives' moderate Reform Bill for England and Wales met with serious Liberal and Radical opposition, Disraeli persuaded the Cabinet to remodel it on popular lines. Three Ministers resigned in protest and, thus further weakened, Disraeli came to accept far-reaching Opposition amendments to the Bill which, contrary to Conservative principles, turned it into a largely democratic measure. The property qualification for the vote was only lowered in the counties, but was abolished in the boroughs where the electorate was now extended to include all male ratepaying householders. Much of the working class thus became enfranchised, and England was halfway towards democracy. Derby now followed Russell into retirement, and in 1868 Disraeli became Prime Minister, left to face the consequences of his action and a confrontation with Gladstone for the next dozen years.

For the Conservatives, the Reform Act was a gamble which

only an astute, progressive policy could turn to advantage. Credit for its popular features, however, went to Bright, and to Gladstone who was now hailed as 'the People's William'. Gladstone acted promptly to reunite his party and consolidate his position as leader. 'I have ever held,' he had said in 1865, 'that it is not the duty of a Minister to be forward in inscribing on the Journals of Parliament his own abstract views, until he conceives the time to be come when he can properly give effect to his opinion.' He now displayed a masterly sense of 'parliamentary timing'. The condition of Ireland had been on his conscience for twenty years, and since 1863 he had been convinced that the Irish State Church was no longer defensible. More recently, the violent activity of an Irish revolutionary society, the Fenians, had revived this national problem. Early in 1868, he persuaded the Commons to pass his resolutions in favour of Irish Church disestablishment and disendowment, and thereby achieved several objects in one move. He reassured the Whigs, who preferred to see the Irish problem settled at the Church's expense rather than the landlords'; he won over the great body of Nonconformists who hoped for Church disestablishment in England and Wales as well; and he gained the alliance of the Irish nationalists. The measure of his achievement was seen at the General Election later in 1868, when the new electorate returned a Liberal majority of over one hundred seats. Gladstone, defeated in Lancashire but elected for Greenwich, was felling a tree in Hawarden park when he received the Queen's summons to the audience at which she was to appoint him Prime Minister. 'My mission,' he said, 'is to pacify Ireland.'

2

The recent disappearance of all the old party leaders and the enlargement of the electorate now made possible the undertaking of reforms which had been neglected for nearly twenty years, and which great changes in that period had rendered essential. Britain needed to overhaul its political, administrative, judicial, social, educational, military, and ecclesiastical systems, if it was to become a modern state capable of holding its own with a united Germany and reunited U.S.A. The Reform Act, which gave political influence to the working-classes and helped to raise their middle-class leaders to power in partnership with the aristocracy, was the first necessary step towards the great reforms demanded. Both the composition and the policy of Gladstone's first Government reflected the new situation.

Gladstone composed his Cabinet with great care. Half its members were Whigs, most of them in the Lords where the Government might be weak; one surviving Peelite, Cardwell, was appointed to the War Office; Lowe's support was secured by his appointment to the Exchequer. The most significant newcomer was Bright, whose reluctance to accept office Gladstone overcame. As a Nonconformist, middle-class industrialist, and popular Radical opposed to the aristocratic system, Bright belonged to a class never previously considered fit for office. But Gladstone was determined to broaden the base of the party by including the democratic Radicals, and later appointed two more of them, W. E. Forster and J. Stansfeld, to the Cabinet. By so doing, he created the Gladstonian Liberal party, as distinct from the previous Whig–Peelite party of Palmerston. Though the new combination was more representative of the nation, the old Whigs and new Radicals had only a limited outlook in common. The dominating personality of Gladstone, who belonged to neither group, usually sufficed to hold them together; he was once described as 'the big umbrella' who covered them all. But he was liable to lose the support of one wing or the other in a crisis that strained his powers of leadership. He always spoke of his first Cabinet as 'one of the best instruments for government that ever were constructed'. It carried out a great programme of reforms such as the country demands in each generation. The credit for these was due to many Ministers besides Gladstone; but he made his own personal contribution in Irish legislation, and his influence was often to be felt in other directions, where compromise between divergent views and interests was necessary. His dynamic leadership against opposition in the Commons and by the Lords made possible a great range of achievements.

The Government was concerned to promote social justice and national efficiency, and sought to meet the needs or demands of different sections of the public as far as it considered practicable. Working-class demands were partly met by a Mines Act, Acts to improve the legal position of Trade Unions, and, against the opposition of the Lords, the Ballot Act to protect the voter by secret ballot at elections. Non-Anglicans were catered for by the abolition of remaining religious tests at the Universities. The first of a series of Acts on the subject helped married women to own property independently of their husbands. National efficiency was furthered by reorganization of the Army, which included abolition of the system whereby officers had to purchase the commissions to which they were appointed; of the Home Civil Service, which was opened to entry by competitive examination in place of political patronage; and of the Law Courts. The creation of a new Ministry, the Local Government Board, and a Public Health Act, improved the prospects of social administration; while a Licensing Act, to control public houses and so, perhaps, reduce drunkenness and foster moral improvement, was passed in 1872. But long before this, the Government had encountered serious difficulty over its education policy, which threatened the party's existence.

Widespread illiteracy could no longer be disregarded in an increasingly technological age, and an improved educational system was necessary for the new electorate. The existing system of public education was incomplete because it was voluntary. Primary schools existed only where private organizations or individuals established them, and attendance was not compulsory. The state provided some money for the training of teachers, but left other provision to private initiative. Since the majority of such schools were of Anglican foundation, and taught the doctrines of the Church of England to all pupils, regardless of the sects to which they belonged, the Nonconformists were especially dissatisfied. In 1869, education reformers and Nonconformists, among whom was a young Birmingham Radical, Joseph Chamberlain, combined to form the National Education League, to agitate for a state system of free, compulsory, universal, nonsectarian elementary education. Many Liberal M.P.s supported the programme, and in 1870 the Government introduced its

Education Bill. Gladstone, who set great store by the role of the
Church in education and had himself personally supported the
voluntary system, thought that the Bill went, if anything, too far
in meeting the League's demands. But many of his supporters
were angry and disappointed at a measure which, though providing for a national system of primary schools, did not make
public education free, and incorporated the Church schools in the
new structure. The Government carried the measure against its
party rebels only with the aid of the Conservative Opposition, and
Gladstone found that he had seriously antagonized a big section
of his supporters. He was to do so again.

Gladstone's own political programme included not only the old
Liberal policy of 'peace, retrenchment, and reform', but also a
completely fresh approach to the Irish problem, which he, almost
alone among English statesmen, regarded as of first importance.
He now attempted a radical revision of Anglo-Irish relationships
which he had long pondered, and which he hoped would reconcile Irish nationalist opinion to remaining within the Union established in 1800 against its will. As soon as the Government was
formed, he started to apply his political axe to what he called 'the
triple upas-tree' of Irish discontent with ecclesiastical, agrarian,
and educational conditions.

The Church of Ireland was the established State Church of the
country, legally privileged and richly endowed, as was the Anglican Church in England and Wales. But, a Protestant episcopal
church, it ministered to only a tenth of the Irish population, the
bulk of which comprised a majority of Roman Catholics and a
minority of Nonconformists. Fortified by his electoral victory on
the issue, Gladstone was able in 1869, after considerable opposition in the Lords, to pass his Act, disestablishing the Irish
Church. This was reduced to equality with other churches in Ireland by the loss of its privileges, and of most of its endowments
which were diverted to other Irish needs. The very greatness of
his success, however, contained the seeds of future disadvantage.
By meeting Irish demands, he began to weaken the Irish need for
alliance with the Liberals; while he soon disappointed many

Liberals when he made clear that Irish disestablishment would not be followed by disestablishment in England and Wales.

In 1870, however, his position was still strong enough to secure his second remedial Irish measure, the Land Act. The greater part of Irish soil was owned by a small number of Anglo-Irish landlords who were often absentees, living in England and exploiting their native Irish tenants, most of whom were not protected, like English tenant-farmers, against excessive rents and the danger of ruthless eviction when these were not paid.[1] This agrarian problem was responsible for much Irish poverty, discontent, and terrorist activity which could only be restrained by Coercion Acts giving the Government special powers of repression. It was also a problem harder to solve than the Church. It involved the interests of many landowners, especially in the House of Lords, whose attitude was that of Palmerston, himself an absentee Irish landlord: 'Tenant-right is landlord-wrong.' Gladstone's Act, therefore, was able to touch only the fringe of the problem. It could stop 'exorbitant', but not excessive, rents, thus somewhat improving the tenant farmer's security of tenure; and to a limited extent it offered him financial assistance if he could purchase his holding. Restricted in scope though it had to be, the Act was a great pioneering achievement, due to Gladstone's vision, courage and initiative.

His further attempts at Irish conciliation were both wholly unsuccessful. Hoping to reconcile Ireland to the monarchy, he tried for many months to persuade Queen Victoria to establish the Prince of Wales as a Viceroy resident in Dublin, but as he continued to press her against her repeated refusals, he succeeded only in antagonizing her. Then, in 1873, he tried to create a new University in Dublin which would not be associated with the Protestant ascendancy, as was Trinity College there. The Irish Roman Catholic hierarchy with which, through his old Oxford friend Manning, now Archbishop of Westminster, he had established a good working alliance, obliged him either to provide for

[1] Parliamentary Papers published 1874–6 showed that some 1,500 persons owned two thirds of the total acreage of Ireland. About the same number owned over half of England and Wales, while fewer than 1,700 owned nine-tenths of Scotland.

purely Catholic teaching in a number of subjects or to exclude them from the University. This sectarian issue aroused such opposition in the Liberal party that he had to withdraw the project, and the Government temporarily collapsed. Disraeli, who had described the Ministers as 'exhausted volcanoes', would not consider taking office yet, and left the Liberals to aggravate their internal dissensions to which the Government's measures had given rise.

The achievement of the great reform programme had been made possible by the Government's consistent pursuit of a peaceful policy abroad. Lord Clarendon was Foreign Secretary until his death in 1870, when Lord Granville succeeded him. Gladstone got on well with both, but especially with Granville, who was his closest personal friend among the Whigs, and henceforth led the Liberals in the Lords. He followed Gladstone's lead until his death twenty years later. Though not an outstanding statesman, Granville was invaluable as a link between Gladstone and their aristocratic supporters, whom he deftly soothed and managed, and whose feelings Gladstone, despite his natural courtesy, sometimes ruffled with his forthright sincerity of purpose. Gladstone had his own views on foreign policy, and expounded these to the Cabinet, but he never pressed them against Granville's expert judgement. The Cabinet, which contained a Quaker pacifist in Bright, was generally as peace-loving as Gladstone and Granville. When the Franco-Prussian war broke out in 1870, the Government demanded and received from both belligerents an undertaking to respect the neutrality of Belgium, which it regarded as the only British interest involved. When, soon after, Russia denounced the Black Sea demilitarization clauses of the 1856 Treaty of Paris, the Government in 1871 summoned to London a Conference of the Treaty's signatories which condemned unilateral denunciations of treaties, and then agreed to Russia's action. In 1872, the Government at last ended the possibility of war with the U.S.A. by accepting an international arbitration award whereby it agreed to pay over £3,000,000 in compensation for the depredations of the *Alabama* nearly ten years earlier.

The Government's policy was neither pacifist nor unpatriotic; it was based upon humanity and common sense, and preserved essential British interests. Both the strength and weakness of Gladstone's moral attitude in international affairs were revealed in 1871, when Germany took Alsace from France by right of conquest. He was shocked by a transfer of territory which did not consult the wishes of the inhabitants, and rightly foresaw the seeds of a future war in it. But his own view, that the disputed province might be converted into a separate buffer state, like Belgium, was impracticable, since both France and Germany wanted it; and Granville refused to take up the suggestion.

Peace, prosperity, and government economy made possible further reductions in taxation. In 1873 Gladstone replaced Lowe at the Exchequer, while remaining Premier, and decided that the prospective Budget surplus for 1874 would permit the abolition of the Income Tax, now reduced to $3d.$ in the $£.$ Since the Government could make no further progress in the existing Parliament, it was decided to dissolve and seek a fresh mandate at a General Election. The result, in January 1874, was disastrous. The Irish and the Nonconformists were disappointed by the Government's record, while vested interests were offended by its reforms at their expense: in particular, many election committees did their business in taverns where publicans were hostile to the Licensing Act. 'We have been borne down in a torrent of gin and beer,' Gladstone complained afterwards. He himself made the abolition of Income Tax the chief feature of his programme, but this hardly affected the mass of electors who were not liable to pay it; and the Radical Chamberlain denounced the proposal as mean and 'simply an appeal to the selfishness of the middle class'. As so often, Gladstone suffered from his concentration upon one big idea, to the exclusion of others equally important. The disunited party had no agreed programme to offer the electorate, which returned a Conservative majority of fifty. The Government resigned, and Disraeli became Prime Minister.

3

Disraeli was the opposite of Gladstone in every important respect save one—political courage; and Gladstone readily acknowledged this quality in his opponent—'Disraeli is a man who is *never beaten*.' For the rest, he considered him a cynical, unprincipled adventurer, who could not distinguish between truth and falsehood and who had lowered standards in public life. Some Conservatives thought much the same, but continued to follow him for lack of any other leader. Disraeli had imagination of a different order from Gladstone's; his political vision embraced principally such matters as race, social reform, and imperial grandeur, none of which excited Gladstone's sympathies. Now aged seventy, and five years older than Gladstone, he commanded a party majority for the only time in his life, and had the chance to realize his long frustrated aspirations.

At first, Gladstone was too deeply mortified by the Liberal defeat to wish to carry on the struggle even against Disraeli, and felt that his career was at an end. Oppressed by a sense of failure, and of having misjudged the people whose hero he had previously been, he again doubted his wisdom in choosing a political career, and his fitness for the management of mundane affairs. 'The welfare of my fellow-creatures,' he had recently said, 'is more than ever at stake, but not within the walls of Parliament. The battle is to be fought within the region of thought, and the issue is belief or disbelief in the unseen world.' It was his preoccupation with moral issues in politics which sustained him, and now the new democracy appeared to prefer the immoral Disraeli to himself. He spent much of the year writing articles on Homer, and a book, *The Vatican Decrees,* which examined critically the Roman Catholic doctrine of Papal Infallibility promulgated in 1870. Early in 1875 he resigned the party leadership, which now passed to Granville, while another Whig, Lord Hartington, led the Liberals in the Commons. Thus freed of responsibility, he turned to his theological studies, the better to prepare himself for his last years —which, throughout life, he regarded as possibly not far off.

Though only a private M.P. again, Gladstone could not easily abandon his active interest in politics. Soon enough, in 1875, he criticized Disraeli's purchase of Suez Canal shares without previous authorization by Parliament, and later attacked the Government's financial policy. When the Budget reduced the Income Tax instead of abolishing it, he denounced it as 'socialistic'. He feared that the Income Tax, chiefly paid by the propertied classes, would be exploited in future by unscrupulous demagogic politicians as they sought to obtain the votes of the unpropertied voters with promises of expensive social reforms; and he demanded in the Commons that the retention of the tax should not be given 'a scintilla of countenance'. His appeal failed, and he lamented the failure for the rest of his life. Gladstone always opposed the doctrine of socialism, while remaining most insistent that the poorer classes should be enabled to earn a fair share of the national wealth which they helped to create. He regarded freedom for individual effort as morally superior to state intervention : men and women should rely upon self-help, not the State, to improve their lot, and those who were successful had the duty to assist those who were not. He was wholly sincere in holding these views of personal responsibility for welfare. He himself was exceptionally industrious and thrifty and, in his later years, gave away much of his wealth in charity. On this issue he was doomed to fight a losing battle, as public opinion came increasingly to realize, from experience, that self-help and charity by themselves did not provide the whole answer to the problem of poverty. More immediately, however, a political crisis now occurred, which soon divided public opinion, and enabled him to re-enter national politics and recover his moral ascendancy over the electorate.

In 1875, south-east Europe was disturbed by nationalist outbreaks attempting to liberate the largely Christian population of the Balkan provinces under Turkish rule. In the course of repressing these, the Turks quelled the revolt in Bulgaria by massacres of such brutality as to arouse strong public protest in England. Disraeli denied the atrocities, and adopted a pro-Turkish policy as essential to British interests in the East. When Russia, Austria, and Germany sought to intervene with Turkey, he refused at first to act with them, as he mistrusted Russian intentions; and he thus rendered a peaceful international solution of the Eastern Question less likely. After a long, internal struggle, Gladstone decided that here were three great moral issues which he could not disregard :

humanitarianism, national freedom, and international peace. Encouraged by protests of moral indignation among the public, and by large Liberal deputations which now began to call on him at Hawarden, he published in 1876 a long pamphlet, *The Bulgarian Horrors and the Question of the East*. In this he demanded that the Government should work in concert with the other European powers to liberate Bulgaria from the Turks who 'one and all, bag and baggage, shall I hope clear out from the province they have desolated and profaned'.

The pamphlet sold in great numbers and intensified the agitation, which Gladstone now joined on the public platform. 'Good ends,' he said, 'can rarely be attained in politics without passion'; and for eighteen months he spoke with passionate eloquence at monster meetings throughout the country, and in Parliament, denouncing Turkey and the British Government with equal fervour. By comparison, most of the leading Liberals appeared lukewarm and ineffective, and Gladstone looked increasingly to the Radical section of the party for support. In 1877 he accepted from Chamberlain, recently elected M.P., an invitation to go to Birmingham and inaugurate the National Liberal Federation, a new type of party organization, under popular Radical control, for which he ordinarily had no liking. But he could not afford to be particular, for at this point Russia went to war with Turkey, and a renewal of the Crimean War seemed threatened. He redoubled his agitation until, to his relief, Lord Salisbury, whom he greatly respected, became Foreign Secretary, and was able by skilful diplomacy to prevent the war spreading. The liberation of Bulgaria, on terms disappointing to Russia, was partly achieved at the Congress of Berlin in 1878, when Disraeli claimed to have won peace with honour.

For the moment, the Government was more popular than Gladstone, who suffered the indignity of having his windows smashed by the London mob. But he had not set out to court easy popularity. He now decided he must continue in public opposition to Disraeli's whole policy of government—or 'Beaconsfieldism' as he called it, since Disraeli had been created Earl of Beaconsfield—and attempt, with popular support, to discredit and

destroy his old opponent's extravagant doctrine of imperial prestige and expansion, which condoned oppression abroad, and in-
curred the risk of unjustified war, with a consequent increase in
hardship at home. His opportunity came in 1879 when, with the
country suffering from a severe economic depression, the Government involved it in unsuccessful wars in South Africa and
Afghanistan. Gladstone now accepted the suggestion sponsored
by a local young Liberal peer, Lord Rosebery, to become candidate for the Scottish seat of Midlothian, in order to win it from
the Conservatives. Regarding his new campaign as 'a great and
high election of God', as the General Election of 1880 approached
he turned his electoral contest into a national crusade for peace,
economy, and good government, which seemed to eclipse in ele-
mental force even his Bulgarian agitation. With his vision of a free
and law-abiding community of nations before him, he defined his
principles of foreign and imperial policy in opposition to
'Beaconsfieldism': that the preservation of peace is a paramount
responsibility; that war is only justified if it serves a moral purpose; that the interests of any one state must be subordinate to
those of the community of nations; that prestige and aggrandisement are not the legitimate interest of any state; 'to foster the
strength of the Empire and to reserve it for great and worthy
occasions'; and avoid entangling alliances.

As the thunder of Gladstone's oratory rolled upon unnumbered
audiences, its lightning flashes exposed every possible mistake
attributable to the Government. Something of the impact made
by his 'Midlothian campaign' upon the ordinary elector was described by a journalist who experienced it at one meeting in
London. 'Never shall I, an unenthusiastic non-party man, forget
those tones. Surrendering myself to the prevalent sentiment, it
seemed to me as if someone had touched the stops of a mighty
organ, that searched us through and through. Two more sentences, and we were fairly launched upon a sea of passion. In that
torrent of emotion, the petty politics of the hour figured as huge
first principles, and the opinions of the people became the edicts
of eternity.... All through a speech of long tortuous sentences he
endowed us with a faculty of apprehension we did not know we

possessed. And then the peroration: "You are shortly to pronounce your verdict, you and the people of these isles; and, whatever that verdict may be, as I hope it will be the true one, I trust it will be clear." We leaped to our feet and cheered. "I trust it will be emphatic." We waved our sticks and hats in emphasis. "I trust it will be decisive, and that it will ring" (here, with a swing of the arm clear round his neck, and a superb uplifting of the whole frame, he sent his trumpet voice into every cranny of the hall till it rang again) "from John o'Groats to the Land's End"; and a frantic mass of humanity roared themselves hoarse for a full two minutes.'

At the election in 1880, Gladstone won Midlothian, which he retained for the rest of his career. His campaign, aided by the improved constituency organization of Chamberlain's National Liberal Federation, enabled the Liberals to gain a majority of over one hundred seats. The Conservative Government immediately resigned, and the Queen sent for Hartington and Granville. Neither could form a Government without Gladstone, or be Premier in his place. A landslide victory had restored the leadership to him, and he was now summoned to form his second Ministry.

5

THE GRAND OLD MAN

I

A PROMINENT young Conservative in the new Parliament, Arthur Balfour, nephew of Mrs. Gladstone and of Salisbury, once described Gladstone, whom he admired, as 'in everything except essentials, a tremendous Tory'. The accuracy of the description was never more clearly demonstrated than in his second Government. Gladstone's personal conservatism of habit, and loyalty to individuals and institutions associated with his earlier career, now led him to compose his second Cabinet on the same lines as the first. Again, half the Ministers were Whigs, and only three were

Radicals—Bright, Forster, and a militant newcomer in Chamberlain. As in 1873, Gladstone was for a period Chancellor of the Exchequer as well as Premier. Like the first, this Government lasted five years and then collapsed in disruption. There the resemblance ended, for much had changed since 1874. The recent economic depression gave rise to a new socialist movement and renewed unrest in Ireland; imperial expansion, revived by Disraeli, persisted, and was followed by other countries; the Conservatives felt not only disappointment at their defeat but also an embitterment, after the unrestrained assault of the Midlothian campaign, which long survived Disraeli's death in 1881. National opinion divided more sharply than before on party lines and, while Liberals now hailed Gladstone as 'the Grand Old Man', Conservatives and the upper classes came increasingly to regard him as a danger to society and the Constitution.

No one held this latter view with greater conviction than did Queen Victoria, who now became a permanent stumbling-block for every Liberal Government. In earlier years she had respected and admired Gladstone; during his first Government she had often assisted him and, except over the Irish vice-royalty, had assented to his policies even when she disagreed with them; now she became his perpetual critic and opponent. Since 1874, she had come to identify herself with Disraeli and his policy and, like many others, was appalled by Gladstone's popular agitation against the Government, especially on an issue of foreign policy and imperial security. In earlier years, before 1867, when he himself disapproved of it, such agitation had been conducted only by Radicals like Cobden and Bright, who were regarded as irresponsible demagogues and not national statesmen. Gladstone, always prone to be excitable and impulsive, publicly admitted he had been driven to 'play the part of an agitator', and had certainly overstepped the mark on occasion in his recent campaign. One of his first official acts in 1880 was to apologize to the Austrian Government for his public statement before the Election that no one could point to any spot on the map and say 'there Austria did good'. It was an inept statement from one who preached friendly collaboration between states, and he confirmed his critics' misgivings when he explained that he had made it while 'in a position of greater freedom and less responsibility'. The Queen, as prone as Gladstone to excitability but sometimes less well able to control it, now saw her Prime Minister as a 'half-mad firebrand' and a public danger, whom it was her constitutional duty to control and frustrate while she worked for the restoration of a 'true Liberal feeling' such as moderate Conservatives could accept. He bore patiently with her opposition, though it added greatly to his difficulties. 'The Queen alone is enough to kill a man,' he complained to Rosebery. But he said nothing in public, lest it damage the throne. He was deeply loyal to the monarchy, and always defended it implacably against the republicanism of some of his Radical followers; it was, he said, 'the most illustrious in the world'. He enjoyed the esteem of the Prince of Wales, but never regained the confidence of the Queen. His combination of firmness and old-world courtesy was too heavy and elaborate to ingratiate him with her as Disraeli's insinuating flattery had done. 'Now, contrary to your ways, do pet the Queen,' Mrs. Gladstone had once advised him; but his sincerity of purpose never allowed him to act out of character when dealing with persons and, as he said, 'I cannot play the courtier.' So, to his distress, misunderstanding and mistrust prevailed between them.

Weakened by royal opposition, the authority of Gladstone's renewed leadership in the party and Government was further compromised by the uncertainty of his own future. He had come out of retirement to 'counterwork Lord Beaconsfield', but with no clear intention of returning permanently to political life. He expected, as did most others, that he would retain office long enough to reverse Conservative policy, and then retire for good. He had no other specific policy to offer, and his colleagues tended to divide the Cabinet, as they pressed their own policies in rivalry with one another, against the day when a new candidate would be required for the vacant leadership. In this situation, the position of the forceful, ambitious Chamberlain became increasingly like that of Gladstone in the ageing Palmerston's Cabinet twenty years earlier, and produced much the same atmosphere of mutual distrust and antagonism.

The reversal of 'Beaconsfieldism' proved to be less easy than expected, partly because the clock could not be turned back to 1874, and still more because new, unforeseen issues arose, which distracted the Ministry and sometimes drove it farther along the path it wished to abandon. In many ways, it was able to live up to its promises and Liberal reputation. In his two years at the Exchequer, Gladstone reduced public expenditure, and abolished the Malt tax for the relief of the depressed agricultural industry; but he could not abolish or reduce the Income Tax. Peace was made in Afghanistan. Turkey was compelled to observe the Berlin settlement. War with the Boers in South Africa, which there was hardly time to prevent, broke out in 1880, but was ended in 1881, without consideration of prestige, after the Boer victory of Majuba. Political reform was resumed in 1883, when the Corrupt and Illegal Practices Act outlawed electoral bribery, and so drastically reduced legal election expenses as to enable poor men to stand for Parliament. Democracy was further extended in 1884–5 when two Reform Acts were passed. These extended the vote, as given to the English boroughs in 1867, to householders of all counties (including Ireland) and, for the first time, made nearly all constituencies of equal size. Opposition by the Lords to these measures provoked a great Radical agitation to 'mend or end' the House of Lords with which Gladstone had little sympathy. As always, he strenuously defended the Commons in its clash with the Lords, but had no wish to set about reforming the Upper House as well. The Queen, who desired even more to preserve the Lords, intervened to bring him and the Conservative leader Salisbury into conference, and they reached an agreed compromise (in which, to Gladstone's relief, the University constituencies were preserved). 'It is my singular fate,' he told Granville, 'to love the antiquities of our constitution much more even than the average Tory;' and his willingness to compromise, in order to resolve the conflict, again disappointed the Radicals.

Abroad, 'Beaconsfieldism' had been swiftly reversed for the benefit of Afghans and Boers in 1880–1, but thereafter the Government appeared itself to revert to the imperial policy which it professed to detest, notably in the case of Egypt. Here, the

Khedive Ismail had borrowed heavily from European countries, including England, in his efforts to develop his country. His corrupt and inefficient government made it difficult for him to pay the interest charges on these loans and, though he sold his Suez Canal shares in 1875, he became bankrupt in 1877; he was soon afterwards driven to abdicate by Britain and France, who installed agents in Cairo to supervise Egyptian finances and ensure debt repayments. This intervention provoked a popular nationalist movement, led by a Colonel Arabi, which soon endangered the lives and property of foreigners in Egypt. As a measure of protection, the British fleet was sent in 1882 to Alexandria, where it bombarded the harbour fortifications. This action caused the resignation from the Government of Bright, who embarrassed Gladstone by leaving on grounds of moral objection to it. In this case, as in 1854, Gladstone had decided that violence must be restrained by force. The action was quickly followed by the dispatch of a British army, which later in the year destroyed Arabi's forces at Tel-el-Kebir; and then by the establishment of a British protectorate in Egypt, which was expected to be temporary. In Gladstone's eyes this was justified, because he regarded Egypt as a defaulting debtor state which must be made to honour its financial obligations. He failed to recognize the genuine nature of Egyptian nationalism, greatly though he sympathized with the movements of peoples 'rightly struggling to be free' elsewhere. Soon enough, he was shocked to discover the poverty and oppression suffered by the Egyptian peasantry, which made him more than ever anxious to evacuate Egypt as soon as orderly government was restored.

Popular though the victory of Tel-el-Kebir was at home, the Government was embarrassed at appearing to emulate Palmerston and Disraeli, and determined not to accept responsibility for Egypt's southern province, the Sudan. This contained Egyptian garrisons which they decided should be withdrawn, to avoid war with a popular leader, the 'Mahdi', who led the hostile Sudanese forces. To undertake the evacuation of the Sudan garrisons, a committee of the Cabinet, in Gladstone's absence but with his assent, selected General Gordon. Gladstone once described

Gordon as 'a hero of heroes', and he was a popular national figure who, however, proved not to be a satisfactory choice for the task. Arrived in the Sudan, Gordon decided it was necessary to 'smash the Mahdi', and remained at Khartoum where, in the absence of reliable communications, his position soon became endangered. Gladstone complained that Gordon had been sent to evacuate the Sudan and then required the British Army to evacuate him. Slowly and reluctantly the Government agreed to send a relief force, while Gladstone fended off criticism at delay by describing Gordon as not surrounded but only hemmed in at Khartoum. In January 1885 the force reached Khartoum, only to find it had been stormed, and Gordon killed, two days earlier.

The Government's unpopularity at this disaster, which was openly condemned by the Queen, hastened a collapse already threatened by internal differences. Its reputation was hardly redeemed by a sudden demand for a £10,000,000 War Credit to deter Russia from advancing towards Afghanistan. It resigned in June, and was succeeded by a minority Conservative Government under Salisbury, pending the prospective General Election to be held under the Reform Acts. The Radicals, led by Chamberlain, published their manifesto in *The Unauthorised Programme*—so called because it was independent of the predominantly Whig Cabinet and the septuagenarian Gladstone, upon whom it virtually served notice to quit. But Gladstone was already turning his mind to a new and final solution of the biggest single problem with which the Government had been grappling for five years, and which threatened to convulse the whole United Kingdom.

2

In an election manifesto in 1879, Disraeli had drawn attention to the revival of Irish unrest as the most serious problem demanding treatment. Catholic Emancipation, the Famine, Liberal legislation in 1869–70, had all failed to break Irish nationalists' opposition to the Union which had deprived Ireland of its Parliament in Dublin and the measure of self-government extorted from England in 1782. After 1800, Ireland remained one of the worst-governed provinces in Europe, much in the condition of a neglected colony where the impoverished natives could only express their needs by violence and be ruled by coercion. Gladstone's first mission to pacify Ireland had left as many grievances as it removed, and as early as 1873 Isaac Butt, the moderate Irish parliamentary leader, had started to organize a new movement for Irish 'Home Rule'. After 1877, when Ireland was suffering from the worst famine in thirty years, Butt was succeeded as leader of the Irish parliamentary party by Charles Stuart Parnell, a young Protestant Irish landowner, of Anglo-American parentage, whose hostility to British rule made him determined to secure Home Rule by any method that came to hand. He soon received in Ireland the sort of veneration which Gladstone enjoyed in Britain, and was able to organize his party with a rigid discipline not previously known in British politics. For several years he harassed governments with systematic obstruction in parliamentary debates which brought business to a standstill. But he was even more dangerous when he worked in alliance with the Irish Land League which the nationalist Michael Davitt had formed, in 1879, to restrain oppression by landlords.

The Land League was the peasants' response to a recent deterioration of their already depressed condition. Cheap American corn, unimpeded under Free Trade, was now beginning to enter the United Kingdom in such quantities that home agriculture was being progressively undersold and ruined. In Ireland, a country almost wholly occupied in agriculture, landlords continued to demand rents which their tenants became increasingly unable to pay; and the rate of evictions for non-payment of rent rose rapidly. By 1880, the situation was becoming politically, socially, and economically desperate. Now called upon to renew his mission, Gladstone's first action was to introduce in 1880 a Bill providing compensation to peasants evicted for non-payment of rent after two bad harvests. The Bill was rejected by the Lords, where many Whigs voted against the Government and one, Lord Lansdowne, resigned from it, in protest against such interference with the rights of private property. The Lords' action aggravated the situation in Ireland, where violence and outrages increased with the number of evictions. Gladstone was now moved to apply a more radical remedy. In 1881, almost single-handed, he drew up and piloted through Parliament an immense, far-reaching Land Act which gave the Irish tenant-farmers fair rents, fixity of tenure in their tenancies, and the right to free sale of these. With the 'three Fs' and renewed state assistance for the purchase of holdings he managed to establish a dual ownership of the soil between landlord and tenant, and so launched a beneficial agrarian revolution in Ireland. At the same time, he had to pass a severe Coercion Act, to repress outrages and to reconcile the House of Lords to the Land Act. But he failed to reconcile the Whig Duke of Argyll, who resigned from the Cabinet in protest against interference with landlords' rights. Neither measure did anything to abate the demand for Home Rule, and the obstructive Parnell himself suffered coercion when he was arrested and imprisoned in Dublin. He was released in 1882, when he was prepared to collaborate in helping the operation of the Land Act, now to be supplemented by a new measure to relieve arrears of rent, and it seemed that a fresh start in Anglo-Irish relations had been made. Gladstone now appointed as Irish Secretary Lord Frederick Cavendish, Hartington's brother and his own nephew by marriage. The day after he arrived in Dublin Lord Frederick was assassinated by terrorists, and a stricken Gladstone had to agree to a yet harsher Coercion Act to avert anarchy.

Since 1871, Gladstone had never denounced Home Rule, though he had opposed it while he felt able to provide an alternative remedy. Irish intransigence and unrest increasingly aroused his doubts about an acceptable alternative. When, in 1885, the Cabinet considered a big scheme of local self-government for Ireland which fell short of Home Rule, Gladstone and Chamberlain favoured this, but Hartington did not; the Ministers were still divided when they resigned in the summer. Gladstone now began discreetly to sound some of his colleagues for their views on Home Rule but, perhaps unwisely, refrained from confiding in Chamberlain. At the same time, Parnell secretly approached some Conservatives on the subject and felt so encouraged that, at the General Election in the autumn, he advised Irish voters who had no Nationalist candidate to vote Conservative instead of Liberal.

The results of the Election were startling. The Liberals made great gains in the English counties, and won a majority of eighty-six over the Conservatives; but they lost every seat in Ireland, which returned eighty-six Home Rulers. Parnell's tactics had cost the Liberals twenty or more seats, and left him holding the balance between the English parties. The overwhelming Irish vote for Home Rule convinced Gladstone that it must be conceded, and he confidentially informed Salisbury that he would support the Government if it made the concession. At this point his son Herbert indiscreetly made public Gladstone's conversion to Home Rule, and thus appeared to saddle the Liberals with responsibility for it. Salisbury, who did not intend to risk splitting his party on the issue, at once ended his political flirtation with Parnell. When the new Parliament met early in 1886, the Irish joined the Liberals in voting against his Government, which then resigned. Gladstone, now summoned to form an alternative Government, found himself in something like Peel's position in 1846.

3

Gladstone had been losing Whig support since 1880, and now Hartington and many moderate Liberals refused to join his new Cabinet, half of which was composed of Radicals. Among these was Chamberlain, who entered it reluctantly. He distrusted Parnell, and wished the Government to concentrate on popular reforms for the whole country, instead of Home Rule which might harm the party and cause Gladstone to remain leader in circumstances unfavourable to radicalism and his own ambitions. Gladstone neither liked nor sympathized with Chamberlain whom he regarded as an untrustworthy upstart, and made no effort to conciliate him. Though he needed both the Radicals' and Whigs' support, he believed that if necessary he could out-match them either in Parliament or the country. He now drew up a Home Rule Bill which provided for a separate government and Parliament in Dublin, with control over nearly all matters except foreign affairs, defence, and the customs tariff; these remained under control by the Westminster Parliament, from which Irish

M.P.s would be excluded. The Bill, which offered more than Parnell had expected, provoked Chamberlain's resignation, and he joined Bright and Hartington in opposing it.

The Commons' final debate on the Bill in June raised political excitement to a height unknown since 1832 or 1846. Gladstone, 'almost as white as the flower in his coat', justified the measure in one of his greatest speeches. 'Ireland,' he pleaded, 'stands at your bar, expectant, hopeful, almost suppliant,' at 'one of the golden moments of our history'; but in vain. Ninety-three Liberals voted with the Conservatives against the Bill, which was defeated by a majority of thirty votes. Gladstone thought neither of resignation nor retirement, and obtained the Queen's permission to appeal at once to the country. To her horror, he now appeared to raise the spectre of class war in his bid for popular support. 'The adverse host,' he told Midlothian, 'consists of class and the dependents of class,' and later added that in all considerations involving 'truth, justice and humanity—upon these, all the world over, I will back the masses against the classes'. More unprepared and precipitate than that of 1874, the Election of 1886 brought him a yet greater defeat. Though the Irish Nationalists and Gladstonian Liberals did win a majority of votes cast, they obtained only a minority of seats, since in many constituencies dissident Liberals and Conservatives stood down in each others' favour, to secure uncontested returns in opposition to Gladstone. The Government resigned, to be succeeded by Salisbury's Conservative Ministry which henceforth had the support of the Liberal Unionists led by Hartington and Chamberlain.

Gladstone's conversion to Home Rule was as complete and final as all his earlier conversions to Liberal policies; but in this case, Home Rule was his own original contribution to liberalism, and to it he dedicated the rest of his life. Sadly, he put aside all thought of the retirement for which he longed (though he was none the less able to produce, in 1890, two more books—*The Impregnable Rock of Holy Scripture*, and *Landmarks of Homeric Study*). Approaching eighty, with the Court, fashionable Society, most of the aristocracy and the propertied and educated classes, and many of his old colleagues ranged against him, he now stood forth, as the leader of an increasingly Radical party with which he had no special sympathy, and on behalf of a national minority who would show no special gratitude, to fight what was largely a one-man crusade. He had no first-hand experience of Ireland which he had visited only once, very briefly, in 1877. But by his personal vision of Home Rule as atonement for English misgovernment of Ireland in the past, Gladstone showed his understanding of the spirit which prompted Irish nationalism. He now had to convert the bulk of English opinion which was not prepared, so far, to do more than remedy existing grievances, and did not consider Home Rule relevant to the relief of prevailing distress.

Salisbury, who said the Irish were as unfitted for self-government as Hottentots, sought to give Ireland resolute government by coercion and, with Balfour, to 'kill Home Rule by kindness', in the shape of further land reforms to create peasant proprietors in place of tenants. This was an extension of Gladstone's previous remedy; but the Conservatives also exploited the very real division between Protestant and Catholic in Ireland, especially in Ulster, which Gladstone underestimated when he treated the 'Irish nation' as one people. The Irish accepted the reforms but resisted coercion, which reinforced the demand for Home Rule. The harshness of coercion was continually exposed by Gladstone and his Liberals, and their campaign steadily made progress. The National Liberal Federation had deserted Chamberlain for Gladstone; a number of Liberal Unionists returned to the party, which began to win by-elections throughout the country.

Gladstone was anxious to win not only a majority for Home Rule, but also an English majority which, being independent of Irish votes, would give the Lords no excuse for rejecting his next Bill after it passed the Commons. He had to win over what Rosebery called 'the predominant partner' in the Union. His growing success in this direction was abruptly halted, in 1890, when Parnell appeared in court as party to a divorce case, in circumstances which appeared gravely to damage his personal reputation. Gladstone was a puritan but not a prig, and refused to condemn Parnell in a matter of private morality. But he was re-

luctantly convinced by his colleagues that he must politically dis-
sociate himself from Parnell, if public support for Home Rule
was not to be lost. He therefore recommended Parnell to retire
temporarily from the Irish leadership until the storm of public
disapproval blew over. Parnell was too proud and self-confident to
do so and, by seeking to retain his position, divided the Irish party
into two bitter factions which survived his death in 1891. The
conduct of the 'uncrowned king of Ireland' dashed Liberal hopes
of success. At the General Election of 1892, the Gladstonian
Liberals were left still in a minority against the Unionist parties,
and had a majority of only forty seats in the new House with the
addition of the Irish Nationalists.

Gladstone, after an interview with the Queen which he likened
to 'such as took place between Marie Antionette and her execu-
tioner', now formed his fourth Government. Unlike its predeces-
sors, it contained only a small minority who were either Whigs or
in the Lords; and, at the age of eighty-three, he found himself
entertaining many semi-socialist demands in the party programme which he would earlier have refused to countenance. But
he subordinated every personal consideration to the necessity of
his second Home Rule Bill. The session of 1893, which was the
longest on record, was dominated by this measure, which he
personally piloted through the Commons with undiminished
energy and skill. It passed by a small majority, and was then
rejected by an overwhelming vote in the Lords. His life-long
tenderness towards the peerage thus finally proved unrewarding.

Gladstone wished to fight a fresh Election on the issue, but at
this point most of his Cabinet refused to follow him. They were
younger men who did not share his exclusive dedication to Home
Rule, and who differed from him on other issues. Some of them
favoured the now popular cause of colonial expansion, which he
deplored as 'the lust and love of territory', and one of the 'curses
of mankind'; and they supported the Admiralty's latest demand
for a programme of naval rearmament. To this Gladstone was as
adamantly opposed as he had been thirty years earlier, but now he
did not feel able to continue the struggle. With hearing and eye-
sight at last beginning to fail, and deserted by his colleagues, he

decided upon final retirement. In Marsh 1894 he delivered his last speech in the Commons, where, for the first time in his life, he denounced the House of Lords and foretold its eventual reform; and then handed his resignation to the Queen, who grieved him by thanking him only for his services to the dynasty and not for his sixty years of service to the State.

Rosebery succeeded him as Premier, and what had been the last Gladstone government survived a year without Gladstone, until its defeat and resignation in 1895. A year later, renewed atrocities by the Turks, this time in Armenia, drew Gladstone from retirement to make a public speech of protest, in Liverpool where he had first addressed Canning over eighty years earlier. As he passed through the crowded streets to give his last message, says one of his biographers in the words of Homer, 'he beheld again the wonder of the common man gazing upon him as upon a god'. This gaze was renewed for the last time two years later. After his death on 19 May 1898, his body lay in state at Westminster where, for two days, a silent crowd passed endlessly by the coffin before it was borne, with the future Kings Edward VII and George V among the pallbearers, to its grave in the Abbey.

4

Viewed superficially, Gladstone's career appears as a series of paradoxes and inconsistencies not easily to be explained or justified; but one fundamental characteristic sufficed to resolve the apparent contradictions and to render him all of a piece. Intellectually a dogmatic churchman, he was spiritually a man with an evangelical conscience to which he made himself accountable for his every thought, word, and deed. He regarded every undertaking in life as a vocation. He entered and remained in politics with misgivings, because he realized the competing claims of material interests and spiritual values. But, like Milton, he could 'not praise a fugitive and cloistered virtue'; and he retained his integrity because, more successfully than many, he followed the Christian precept to be as wise as the serpent and harmless as the dove.

In the rough and tumble of politics he often encountered disappointment, but his faith, courage, and sanguine temperament sustained him. 'Men', he said, 'have no business to talk of disenchantment; ideals are never realized.' He did not die embittered, though he was oppressed by black forebodings for the future. At the end, he felt perplexity rather than doubt when he affirmed 'I am thankful to have borne a great part in the emancipating process of the last sixty years, but entirely uncertain how, had I now to begin my life, I could face the problems of the next sixty years.' But, he added, 'of one thing I am, and always have been, convinced—it is not by the State that men can be regenerated and the terrible woes of this darkened world be effectually dealt with.'

For him government came to mean self-government, but not in the political sense alone: every one was responsible for government of self, as well as being his brother's keeper. He took this double responsibility upon himself, and uniquely sought to impress it on the world. When he died, his political opponent Balfour praised him as an irreplaceable genius who had shown democracy, if it was to survive, that 'the mere average of civic virtue' is not enough —'more than that is required; more than that was given us by Mr. Gladstone.' His epitaph might well have been provided by the humble woman who, in May 1898, told her child: 'Mr Gladstone is dead. Things will never be the same again.'

PRINCIPAL DATES

(G. = Gladstone. His election dates indicate General Elections)

1809 Birth of G. at Liverpool. Peninsular War.

1812 Canning M.P. for Liverpool. French retreat from Moscow. Anglo-American War.

1821 G. goes to Eton. Austria crushes Italian risings. Greek War of Independence against Turkey.

1827 G. leaves Eton. Premiership and death of Canning.

1828 G. goes to Oxford. Repeal of Test and Corporation Acts.

1829 Catholic Emancipation Act. Peel loses Oxford by-election.

1830 Accession of William IV. Grey's Whig Government.

1831 G. attacks Reform Bill; graduates with Double First.

1832 1st Reform Act. G. visits Rome; elected M.P. for Newark.

1833 Emancipation Act. The Oxford Movement begins.

1834 Poor Law Act. Peel's first Government. G. Junior Lord of the Treasury.

1835 G. Colonial Under-Secretary; re-elected for Newark. Melbourne's Whig Government. Municipal Reform Act.

1836 G. serves on Parliamentary Committees. Civil Marriage Act.

1837 Accession of Victoria. G. re-elected for Newark. Disraeli enters Parliament. Canadian rebellions.

1838 *The Church in its Relation with the State.* Chartist Movement.

1839 G. marries Catherine Glynne. Durham Report. Anti-Corn Law League.

1840 G. denounces opium traffic and Chinese War.

1841 G. re-elected for Newark; enters Peel's second Government as Vice-President of Board of Trade.

1842 Mines Act. Chartist petition to Parliament.

1843 G. enters the Cabinet. Collapse of O'Connell's Irish nationalist movement.

1844 Factory Act. G.'s Railway Act.

1845 G. resigns over Maynooth Bill. Irish famine begins.

1846 G. Colonial Secretary in Peel's third Government. Repeal of Corn Laws. Russell's Whig Government.

1847 Factory Act. G. elected M.P. for Oxford University.

1848 Last Chartist demonstration. Revolutions in Europe.

1850 Australian Colonies Government Act. Don Pacifico debate. Death of Peel. G. in Naples.

1851 *Letters to Lord Aberdeen.* Dismissal of Palmerston.

1852 Derby's first Government. New Zealand Government Act. G. re-elected for Oxford; Chancellor of Exchequer in Aberdeen's Coalition. Napoleon III establishes Second Empire.

1853 G.'s first Budget. Russo-Turkish War.

1854 Crimean War. Oxford University Reform Act.

1855 G. joins Palmerston's first Government and resigns.

1856 Treaty of Paris ends Crimean War.

1857 G. re-elected for Oxford; opposes China War, and Divorce Act.

1858 *Studies in Homer.* Derby's second Government. G. High Commissioner in Ionian Isles.

1859 Italian war. G. re-elected for Oxford; joins Palmerston's second Government as Chancellor of the Exchequer.

1860 War scare. Cobden's Anglo-French Trade Treaty.

1861 American Civil War. G. repeals Paper Duties; creates Public Accounts Committee.

1862 The *Alabama* sails. G. visits north England; supports Southern Confederacy.

1863 Post Office Savings Bank Act.

1864 Danish War. G. supports parliamentary reform.

1865 Death of Palmerston. Russell Prime Minister. G. elected M.P. for S. Lancashire; Liberal leader in Commons.

1866 Exchequer and Audit Act. Liberal Reform Bill. Derby's third Government. Fenian activity.

1867 Second Reform Act. Confederation of Canada.

1868 Disraeli Prime Minister. G.'s Resolutions on Irish Church; elected M.P. for Greenwich; Prime Minister.

1869 *Juventus Mundi.* Irish Church Act. Suez Canal opened.

1870 First Irish Land Act. Education Act. Civil Service Reform. First Married Women's Property Act. Franco-Prussian War.

1871 Army Reform. Trade Union Act. University Tests Act.

1872 Ballot Act. Licensing Act. Public Health Act. *Alabama* Arbitration Award.

1873 Judicature Act. Irish University Bill. G. resumes the Exchequer.

1874 G. re-elected for Greenwich. Disraeli's second Government. Butt's Home Rule movement.

1875 G. resigns leadership. Suez Canal shares purchased. Trade Union Act. Artisans' Dwellings Act. Parnell enters Parliament.

1876 Near Eastern crisis. *The Bulgarian Horrors and the Question of the East.* Chamberlain enters Parliament.

1877 Russo-Turkish War. G. addresses new National Liberal Federation and many meetings; visits Dublin.

1878 Congress of Berlin. Afghan War begins.

1879 Zulu War. Annexation of Transvaal. Midlothian campaign. Irish Land League.

1880 G. elected M.P. for Midlothian; Prime Minister and Chancellor of Exchequer.

1881 First Boer War. Second Irish Land Act. Coercion Act. Death of Beaconsfield.

1882 Assassination of Lord F. Cavendish. Coercion Act. Arrears of Rent Act. Occupation of Egypt. G. resigns from the Exchequer.

1883 Electoral Corrupt and Illegal Practices Act.

1884 Third Reform Act. Clash with House of Lords.

1885 Death of Gordon. Redistribution Act. Salisbury's first Government. G. re-elected for Midlothian.

1886 G.'s third Government. Liberal split on Home Rule Bill. G. re-elected for Midlothian. Salisbury's second Government.

1887 Irish Coercion Act. Queen Victoria's Jubilee.

1888 Local Government Act. G.'s Home Rule campaign develops.

1890 *The Impregnable Rock of Holy Scripture; Landmarks of Homeric Study.* Ruin of Parnell.

1891 Irish Land Purchase Act. Deaths of Parnell and Granville.

1892 G. re-elected for Midlothian; forms fourth Government.·

1893 Second Home Rule Bill passes the Commons.

1894 Retirement of G. Rosebery Prime Minister.

1896 G. denounces Armenian Atrocities, at Liverpool.

1898 Death of G., 19 May; burial in Westminster Abbey, 28 May. Conquest of the Sudan.

SUGGESTIONS FOR FURTHER READING

THE most comprehensive account of Gladstone, and perhaps the greatest political biography in the English language, is J. Morley's *Life of W. E. Gladstone*, written soon after his death (3 vols., 1903; 2 vol. edition, 1908). This contains many extracts from his speeches and letters. It has influenced all later biographers, whose works are much shorter but often contain fresh material. Among these are G. T. Garrett, *The Two Mr. Gladstones* (1936); E. Eyck, *Gladstone* (1938); J. L. Hammond and M. R. D. Foot, *Gladstone and Liberalism* (1952); P. Magnus, *Gladstone* (1954). A short, lively study is F. Birrell, *Gladstone* (1933).

Since Gladstone attracted most attention after he became famous, his later years are more fully memoirized than the earlier. Reminiscences by close acquaintances, containing important information about his views, conversations, methods, and habits, include A. West, *Private Diaries of Sir A. West* (1922); Lord Kilbracken, Reminiscences (1931), chapters 4 and 5; Rendel, *Personal Papers of Lord Rendel* (1931). Personal recollections and a defence of his father are given in *After Thirty Years* (1928) by Viscount (Herbert) Gladstone. The domestic life is revealed in *Catherine Gladstone* (1919) by her daughter M. Drew; and G. Battiscombe, *Mrs. Gladstone* (1956).

Gladstone speaks for himself in his correspondence in A. Tilney Bassett, *Gladstone to his Wife* (1936), comprising letters from his early years onwards; P. Guedalla, *Gladstone and Palmerston* (1928), and *The Queen and Mr. Gladstone* (2 vols., 1933) of which the Introduction has been separately published in paperback (1958). An edition of the daily diary which Gladstone kept from the age of fourteen is in preparation by M. R. D. Foot.

Books which supply additional background information to some of Gladstone's special interests include (political) R. B. McCallum, *The Liberal Party from Grey to Asquith* (1963); (economic) C. R. Fay, *Great Britain from Adam Smith to the Present Day* (1st edition 1928); (Ireland) N. Mansergh, *The Irish Question* 1840–1921 (new edition 1965); (religious) S. C. Carpenter, *Church and People* 1789–1889 (1933).

INDEX